Dick Simmo

Oct. 1977

Aberdeen, Wn.

Two men and their dogs set out for the hunt in what appears to be promising terrain. Photo: Michigan Conservation Department.

WITH

Luther A. Anderson

Winchester Press

HUNTING THE UPLANDS

SHOTGUN AND RIFLE

Library of Congress Cataloging in Publication Data

Anderson, Luther A
  Hunting the uplands with rifle and shotgun.

  Includes index.
  1. Upland game bird shooting.
  2. Deer hunting.   I. Title.
SK323.A5   799.2'0914'3   77-7196
ISBN 0-87691-191-2

WINCHESTER is a Trademark of Olin Corporation
used by Winchester Press, Inc. under authority and
control of the Trademark Proprietor

Published by Winchester Press
205 East 42nd Street
New York, N.Y. 10017

Printed in the United States of America

Contents

PART TWO　*THE RIFLE*

PART ONE

THE SHOTGUN

1

Hunting the Uplands with Shotgun

The shotgun has a wealth of tradition behind it. Leave aside for a moment those famous squirrel rifles and "Kentucky windage"—we are a nation of shotgunners. We use shotguns for shooting games—trap, skeet, or clay targets out of a hand trap—as well as for game, including everything from small furred or feathered game right up to, given the appropriate ammunition, deer.

But just what is a shotgun? Well, you can define it as a smoothbore gun that throws a pattern of shot when fired, and having a killing range of about 40 to 50 yards for the average hunter (although experts with well-patterned guns can be lethal at 60 yards). Depending upon the gauge of the gun and load used, the shotgun is an excellent arm for all upland game. Shotguns, of course, come in various actions and gauges and have shotshells of varying performances available for them. What selections are made depend largely on the game to be hunted and the equipment the hunter himself prefers. Such preference can only be based on two precepts: what is available, and what has worked well for that hunter in that situation.

Some of the choices include:

The Single Shot

The single shot is the least-expensive type of action available. It is fine for an occasional jaunt in the field and is a good sturdy gun for the beginner.

Most single shots handle nicely, are well balanced, and can stand a lot of abuse. If this is the action selected, make sure that it has a positive and clean ejection of shells. A single shot is simple to operate and is safe for the novice, who has only to snap the gun open to see if a shell is in the chamber and can eject that one shell quickly when necessary.

The single shot also tends to promote accuracy, for with only one shot at the shooter's disposal, he tries harder to make it count.

The Bolt Action

The bolt action is inexpensive, sturdy, and shoots straight. It is the least-expensive repeating shotgun on the market. The bolt rarely gets out of order, can take a beating, and for short hunting trips after small game can be satisfactory. Although clips hold from two to five shells, the bolt action is not fast enough to make a double on a covey rise. It is not the action for the left-handed gunner (there being no left-handed bolts that I know of). Still, it may suffice for general shooting by right-handers.

The Pump Action

Sooner or later the hunter will doubtless want a repeater, one of the most popular of which is the pump or slide-action gun. The pump is durable and fast operating. With up to five shots at quick disposal as fast as the shooter can shoot and shuck, it is a thoroughly practical and sturdy firearm. The first pump action to take hold and be successful was the Winchester Model 1897, which proved the real worth of this type of action in the field.

Manually operated, the pump is rugged, more expensive than a single shot but less than some of the other actions, and handles with ease and assurance. Pump actions have worked out so admirably in the uplands and marshes, and also at such games as trap and skeet, that the pump is probably the most prevalent American shotgun.

Above all, pumps, with their single sighting plane, are easy to get on target fast. They are also available in various styles, both plain and fancy. If you don't like the plain barrel, you can obtain the pump with matted or ventilated ribs, something many trap, skeet, and duck shooters demand.

The Semiautomatic

The semiautomatic or autoloader is often but wrongly called an automatic. The semiautomatic has recently taken giant steps in popularity. Modern autoloaders are fine-looking arms, easy to shoot, and lighter than they used to be. They are, of course, also rapid firing, providing in fact the fastest action of all. Some autoloaders are streamlined in appearance, dependable, and reasonable in price.

As with the pump or any other action, the purpose is to acquire a firearm capable of withstanding years of rugged service while providing dependable performance. Most modern autoloaders nowadays fit this description (some of the older ones tended to jam if subjected to wind-driven sand or dirt). The quality autoloader will fire all of its shots as fast as the trigger is pulled. Ejection is automatic. All you have to do is pull the trigger and the empty shell flies out automatically with the next shell ready to shoot. In other words, the gun does all the work, leaving the shooter free to concentrate on the target and his aim.

Hunting the Uplands with Shotgun

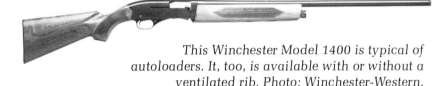

A pump, or slide-action, shotgun provides the shooter with up to five shots as fast as he can operate the action and pull the trigger. This is the Winchester Model 12 with ventilated rib. Photo: Winchester-Western.

This Winchester Model 1400 is typical of autoloaders. It, too, is available with or without a ventilated rib. Photo: Winchester-Western.

The semiautomatic allows the hunter to get off shot after shot faster and more accurately than with other actions, as it gives more time to recover aim and balance after every shot. Muzzle jump and recoil are also reduced considerably in the autoloaders, even with 3-inch Magnum shells.

The Double Barrel

Many a discerning hunter will go for the double barrel, generally considered the crowning achievement of the gunsmith's art. Many of the older doubles, such as a fine L. C. Smith, Parker, or the Winchester Model 21, are valuable collectors' items. But doubles are also still encountered in the field. With either a double trigger or a single, the latter adding to the price of the firearm, the classic side-by-side double is an excellent gun for the uplands. In fact, according to some experts it is the best upland firearm of all.

High-quality doubles, however, are not cheap. To put out a good one requires a great many man-hours, the cost of which

THE SHOTGUN

must be absorbed by the person who buys the finished firearm. Such extras as selective single triggers and selective automatic ejectors, which many double-gun buyers demand, are the result of a lot of intricate and laborious hand labor.

Nonetheless, the fine double is sought after by many hunters. It has an excellent action, is beautiful to handle, and is safe. Open the action and you can see instantly if the gun is loaded or not. Moreover, when it is opened you can safely maneuver fences and other natural or man-made barricades. One barrel is usually bored fairly open for the near shot; the other choked for the next shot farther out. On any kind of game where you seldom get more than two shots anyway, a double may well be your choice.

The Over-Under

The over-under, or superposed, is a vertical double-barreled shotgun. During the past decade or two, the over-under has stepped ahead in popularity with American hunters. Its virtue lies in giving the shooter a single sighting plane, but allowing for more accurate pointing and faster target alignment. Hence, for many shooters the over-under points more naturally than the side-by-side double, handles more surely, and is faster to the mark.

One reason for the precise shooting permitted by this design is that, unlike other shotguns, the shooter's hands are in hori-

Used by almost all serious trap and skeet competition shooters, the over/under is also gaining popularity in the upland-game field. This one is the Winchester Model 101. Photo: Winchester-Western.

Hunting the Uplands with Shotgun

zontal alignment and function together in precise unison. Because of the vertical position of the barrels, the forward hand wraps itself around the lower barrel. With the hands in line, the forward hand higher, the gun can be pointed more accurately. For rapidly crossing targets such as doves or quail, the over-under may be the best action.

Gauge

The gauge of a gun is determined by the number of round, lead balls that the early fowling pieces would accommodate to the pound. The 12 gauge, for instance, held 12 balls, each 0.725 inches in diameter. The 16 gauge held 16 balls, each .665 inches; the 20 gauge 20 balls each .620 inches, and so on.

Many people today consider the 12 gauge the best all-around shotgun if the weight is right. This gauge is a good choice for the shotgunner who wants one gun for any occasion and any game, be it small game, upland birds, waterfowl, or even deer with buckshot or rifled slugs. When shooting the standard field loads of one of the lighter 12s, you will never be overgunned, even when hunting such small game birds as quail or woodcock. Weight and recoil must be kept in mind in selecting a 12—the former a factor if you are carrying the gun all day; the latter if you expect to do a great deal of shooting.

The 16 gauge is a fine upland firearm, but not as popular as it used to be. With the added powder and shot in the magnum load, the 16 competes well with the standard 12 gauge. A 16-gauge gun has less weight than the 12. When equipped with a variable choke, you have a gun that can be used on any upland bird from quail to pheasant, as well as on ducks and geese.

The 20 gauge is a lighter and even handier shotgun than the 16, and is preferred by many. The novice will like the 20 for its fast and easy handling. But any gunner will find that it will kill cleanly and effectively at normal shooting ranges, be the quarry ducks, quail, grouse, or pheasant. The 20-gauge double is one of the favorites in the upland field, and is an excellent beginner's gun. It has a sufficient shot load to do the job and its recoil is light.

The 28 gauge and the .410 caliber are occasionally seen in the field, but they have severe limitations and I can't recommend them for the average hunter. One factor against them is that even the heaviest loads for the 28 and the .410 have one-eighth to one-quarter less shot than the standard 20-gauge load. Beyond 30 yards, their efficiency drops sharply.

Gun Weight

The modern trend is towards lighter guns, especially for upland use. Of course, 12-gauge guns weigh more than the smaller gauges, usually. But even so, you can find 12s weighing 6½ pounds and 20s as little as 5¾ pounds. When you're shopping around for a shotgun, heft various models and choose the most comfortable. Half a pound of weight here or there doesn't make much difference.

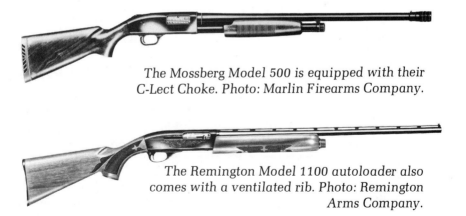

The Mossberg Model 500 is equipped with their C-Lect Choke. Photo: Marlin Firearms Company.

The Remington Model 1100 autoloader also comes with a ventilated rib. Photo: Remington Arms Company.

Hunting the Uplands with Shotgun

Barrel Length

Barrel length is mostly a question of comfort and fit. Usually the longer barrel is best for tall and long-armed men, while the shorter barrel is more suited to shorter persons. Remember that the length of barrel has nothing to do with the gun's range. A long barrel does not drive the pellets faster or farther. The shot charge, as a matter of fact, reaches its highest velocity when it has gone but a short distance up the barrel bore. (A longer barrel such as 30 inches may, however, swing more smoothly for long-range shooting, especially for waterfowl.)

Many shooters also feel that extra length in the barrel allows them to point more accurately. But upland hunters generally lean to the 26-inch barrel, for it comes up faster and does not catch in brush. And because a shorter barrel is lighter, it is also less tiring to carry on an all-day hunt.

Choke

The choke of a gun, found in the muzzle section, constricts the barrel and determines the pattern the gun will throw. The choke thus forms a taper in the muzzle whereby the shot is brought together. Duck and goose hunting, where the shots are usually far out, call for heavy-choke guns with tight patterns. But woods game, such as woodcock, grouse, and quail, demand more of an open bore with wider patterns, because the ranges are usually closer.

The first shotguns were bored true cylinder, or no choke at all, with the result being that the shot spread very wide. With the development of choke, some 100 years ago, shotgun patterns were able to be controlled, thus revolutionizing shotgun shooting.

Shotgun manufacturers vary in their ideas of what constitutes specific choke, however, so the best way to determine your gun pattern is to shoot at the center of a 30-inch circle drawn on a much larger sheet at 40 yards. Then count the number of pellets that enter the target at that distance against the total number of pellets. By and large, the results should be as follows:

Choke	Pattern in Percent
Cylinder	25–35
Improved cylinder	35–45
Modified choke	45–55
Improved modified	55–65
Full choke	65–75

Make sure you choose the choke according to the distance at which most of your game is shot. If this distance is 40 yards or more, you will need a rather constricted choke such as an improved modified or full. But, as most upland game is shot at ranges under 40 yards, a modified choke or improved cylinder will be acceptable for most upland gunners. However, shots at such game as prairie chickens and sharptails will usually be at such long ranges that a full choke may be your best choice.

Get the choke you think is best for your shooting and then try it with different sizes of pellets on your 30-inch circle. Use the shot that patterns best for you.

To give your pump or semiautomatic shotgun versatility, you can add a variable choke or an extra barrel. The addition of a good variable choke will permit you to switch from one choke to another as you see fit. For example, you can change from the modified choke you've been using for quail to an improved modified for hunting pheasant or sharptails at longer ranges.

Variable chokes are made in two different types. One has interchangeable choke tubes, while the other has a collar that can be twisted to change the choke, just as one would adjust the nozzle of a garden hose. One objection to adding a variable choke, however, is that it can change the balance of the gun by adding weight to the end of the barrel.

Hunting the Uplands with Shotgun

Most pump and semiautomatic shotguns are also made so that you can interchange barrels of different chokes and lengths. For example, you can use a long barrel with its long-sighting advantage for hunting waterfowl, and a shorter, quicker-pointing barrel with a more open choke for upland game.

The preferable solution seems to be the addition of an extra barrel, or of a shotgun with replaceable interchangeable choke tubes, but there is no reason why a variable choke will not suffice nicely. In any event, it's cheaper than buying an additional gun.

Gun Fit

The stock of the gun must fit the shooter. To find out how it suits you, shoulder the gun and sight along it. If the gun is right for you, it will come up easily and naturally and you can sight along the barrel with no pressure or distraction. If a mirror is handy, point the gun at the mirror. If you're looking down the barrel, chances are the gun fits you.

One critical measurement is length of stock. This is figured from the trigger to the centerline of the butt and is called the "length of pull." The usual length of pull on factory guns is about 14 inches, which is calculated for the shooter of average height with normal arms and neck. However, you may need more or less pull depending on your height and build.

Following is a rule-of-thumb chart:

Height	Length of Pull in Inches
5' 4"	13½
5' 6"	13⅞
5' 8"	14
5' 10"	14
6'	14¼
6' 2"	14¼
6' 4"	14¾

There are a couple of other aspects of stock fit that must be taken into consideration. These are the drop at comb and the drop at heel. If an imaginary line is drawn from a gun's receiver straight back toward the butt, the drop at comb is the distance from that line to the stock at the comb.

If the comb is too high, the shooter will see too much of the barrel. This will make the gun shoot high. If the comb is too low, the gun will shoot low because the shooter has a tendency to point with the receiver instead of the barrel.

Too thick a comb might produce the same results as too high a comb. A man with very wide cheekbones will need less drop at comb than a man with a narrow face. Trap guns are usually stocked with higher combs than field guns, because the high-shooting qualities become an asset on the trap range on clay targets, which are always rising when they are shot.

A comb that is too high can be lowered by rasping and sanding the stock down to the required height. The stock must then be refinished. The comb can be raised by gluing on doweling or a piece of matching wood, then rasping and sanding down to the needed height. These stock alterations are, of course, best left to a competent gunsmith.

A cheaper and faster way to raise the comb of a shotgun stock is with one of those sleeves with a built-in comb. There are also rubber pads with adhesive bottoms that can be used to raise the drop at the comb. But unfortunately, either of these methods spoils the looks of a fine stock.

Taking once again the imaginary line from receiver to butt, the drop at heel is the distance from the imaginary line to the heel—the top of the stock at the butt end. It is the difference in the drop at the comb and the drop at the heel that determines whether a stock is straight or has too much drop. The straight stock is one in which there is but a little difference between the drop at the comb and the drop at the heel. Experienced shotgunners generally prefer straighter stocks, because they make gun mounting easier and faster. Modern shotguns have much straighter stocks than the guns of yesteryear. Just compare a shotgun built at the turn of the century with one made recently.

Another virtue of a straight stock is that it brings the recoil directly backward. Guns with straighter stocks kick less.

Pitch is still another aspect of shotgun fit. The pitch of a stock is, actually, the angle of the butt. But it is measured from the top of the muzzle to a perpendicular that is placed on the receiver and is at right angles to the butt. Too much pitch makes the gun shoot high; not enough has the opposite effect. The pitch is easily altered by placing paper shims under the butt plate. A shim at the heel (top) will increase the pitch; a shim at the toe (bottom) will decrease the pitch. When the desired pitch is obtained by using shims, the butt end of the stock can be cut at the appropriate angle and the butt plate reinstalled.

The pitch, of course, is relative to the length of the receiver and barrel. If you decide to shorten the barrel on an old 32-inch "Long Tom" pump down to a manageable 26 inches, you will have altered the pitch. Your shooting may be thus affected.

But most frequently, pitch is altered when a rubber recoil pad is installed at home. The same angle may not be kept when the stock is shortened. Gunsmiths and stock makers rarely ever make this mistake.

The average American shotgun stock has a drop at comb of 2½ inches and a drop at heel of 1⅝ inches. The length of pull, as stated before, is 14 inches. Such a stock is designed to fit the average shooter of 5 feet 8 inches to 5 feet 11 inches, and it does so with surprising efficiency. Other persons—taller or shorter, heavier or thinner—are almost certain to need stock alterations if they are going to shoot at their best.

A proper-fitting stock will not make a bad shot suddenly shoot like Rudi Etchen, but it's the first step toward becoming a good shotgunner.

2

Ammunition Highlights

The shotgun shooter who wants to obtain the best results will do well to know the basic facts about the ammunition available for his firearm. Basically, shotgun loads differ in two ways—in amount of powder and shot, and in size of shot. There are further differences in the type of wads used to separate powder from shot, and in the type of powder.

Shotgun Loads

Shotshells are available in magnum loads (high powered), game loads (standard), and field loads. The magnums have a heavier powder and shot charge than either the game or field loads. Magnums, especially in 12 gauge, are packed in 2¾- and 3-inch shells, whereas game and field loads come in 2¾-inch shells. By and large, the 3-inch shells should be reserved for long-range waterfowling. However, they can be superior to game loads for wild turkey and with buckshot for deer. They can even be useful on pheasants when the gaudy ringnecks are flushing wilder than usual.

Some hunters mistakenly select magnums for all their shooting, under the assumption that these shells are superior in all respects. There is little need for these high-powered loads, except for distant shots.

There is no doubt that lighter loads are more pleasant to use. They not only have less kick, which can mean a lot after several hours of intensive shooting, but they're also less noisy and less expensive. For most shotgunning, lighter loads are perfectly adequate. They also tend to tear up the flesh of small birds less. Generally, magnums are best for waterfowl, perhaps turkeys, and furred varmints such as fox. Game and field loads are best for most other game.

Consider the grade and condition of your gun when selecting loads. Some old-time shotguns were made to handle nothing but low-velocity shells. The magnum load in the 12 gauge, for example, is sometimes packed with 4½ drams of powder and 1⅞ ounces of shot—really a powerful load. The standard shell, on the other hand, is loaded with 3¼ drams of powder and 1¼ ounces of shot. It is safe in virtually any type of 12-gauge shotgun.

When using guns of different gauges, keep shells carefully separated before each shooting occasion and recheck them for safety. Shell mix-ups can be dangerous. A 20-gauge shell, for example, will slip up the barrel of a 12-gauge gun and allow a 12-gauge shell to be chambered and fired. The result is curtains.

Shotgun Shells and Sizes

There are five stated designations on a box of shotshells:

1. Gauge—usually noted as 10, 12, 16, 20, 28 gauge, or .410 caliber;

2. Length of shell—noted as 2½", 2¾", 3", or 3½";

3. Powder charge—noted in dram equivalents as 2¾, 3¼, 4½, etc.;

4. Size of shot—noted as 2, 4, 6, 7½, 8, etc.;

5. Charge of shot—noted in ounces as 1, 1⅛, 1¼, etc.

Until recently, all shot was made of lead. But recent federal legislation has made it necessary to manufacture steel shot for waterfowl shooting in some areas. The reason for the switch to steel shot is that ducks ingest lead shot when feeding in marshes and thus die of lead poisoning.

Lead shot today is generally referred to as chilled shot, as opposed to drop shot. This terminology refers to the manufacturing process. Chilled shot is harder than drop shot and consequently has the advantage of not deforming—of not being abraded out of its round shape—as it travels up the shotgun barrel. The fewer the shot that become deformed, the better the pattern. It is deformed shot that fly out of the pattern.

There are, however, some shells made with copper-plated shot used in premium loads—a type of shot with less deformation of pellets than the standard chilled type, and even harder. Steel shot is harder still, but it is highly controversial, more expensive, not available everywhere, and seems to have nothing to recommend it for upland gunning. It should also never be used in older, thin-walled shotguns.

Shot is available in many sizes beginning with No. 00 buckshot and running through No. 9. The smaller pellets, starting with 7½s, usually give their best patterns when driven by lighter powder loads.

All hunters, however, will not conform in their notions about what shot to use for specific game. Some hunters have had success with No. 8s on ruffed grouse, let us say, and will rely on its wider shot pattern for continued success in the field. Other hunters like to use something larger and in which they have greater confidence, like No. 6, for all their grouse shooting.

Local conditions, in addition, may dictate what is best for

certain game species and for the time it is hunted. For example, I do know that when upland birds are not hunted much they tend to flush close. When the pressure is on, they tend to take off at a distance. How far away the game rises often dictates what type of shot will perform best—small for the close-in shots and larger for those at a distance.

Buckshot is used for deer hunting mainly, and rifled slugs are also available. The latter are deadly at short ranges. Spirally grooved to make them spin, rifled slugs are quite accurate up to a maximum of 100 yards in the 12 gauge, and are used quite extensively in some parts of the deer country.

Following is a table of shot sizes recommended for upland game:

Bobwhite quail	7½ to 8	Sharptail	4 to 6
Dove	7½ to 8	Turkey	4 to 6
Pheasant	4 to 6	Western quail	6 to 7½
Prairie chicken	4 to 6	Woodcock	8 to 9
Ruffed grouse	4 to 6	Rabbit	4 to 6
		Squirrel	4 to 6

3

The How-To of Wing Shooting

The upland wingshooter can learn a lot by gunning ducks over water, where he will see the pattern register in the lake or stream. Shoot too high and your pellets hit water over the duck; shoot too low and the shot pattern will strike water under the target. The same happens when shooting behind or in front of the waterfowl. When the ducks are moving, you must take into account that your shot charge has to emerge from the barrel and cross a certain amount of space to the flying target. Meanwhile, with the duck moving, you're not going to connect unless you lead.

In other words, you have to shoot ahead of your flying bird, whether upland or waterfowl. This can be done by using any of three techniques—sustained lead, fast swing, or snap shot.

The sustained lead is used a lot on upland game. In this style, the gunner swings ahead of the bird and at the same speed ahead, and when he thinks his lead is right, presses the trigger.

Showing excellent field form, this hunter approaches his pointing dog gun held high and ready. When the bird flushes, he'll shoulder the gun, simultaneously throwing off the safety, for a quick, sure shot. Photo: Leonard Lee Rue III.

The fast swing is particularly useful for the waterfowler. With this method the gunner swings from behind the bird as it is in the air, passes it, presses the trigger when the lead looks right, and keeps on swinging after the trigger is pulled. The gun swings faster than the bird is traveling, and this is an excellent style for shooting crossing birds and other angled targets, especially at a distance.

The snap-shot system is used especially on upland game, and there is no denying that it is fast. In this style, the gunner pulls the gun to his shoulder, points it directly at the spot he wants to hit, and then fires. He must figure out his target and lead immediately, and press the trigger at the right time. It should work, especially where the bird is seen for only a few seconds, as is the case with most upland game in forested cover.

With the gun bored somewhat open and the bird heading away from the gun, the snap system works well. Some hunters use it all the time. One of its shortcomings, however, is that it does not leave much variation. The flight of the upland bird is mostly irregular, and as the snap shot cannot be corrected, it is chancy.

It is, however, fast. But if you find that you are missing with this style, there is every possibility that a sustained lead or a fast swing will work better for you. Whatever style you choose, once the bird is on the wing there is little time for hesitation. You must make up your mind quickly which style is best, and usually the snap shot will turn the trick.

There are some shots where no lead is required. If it happens that the bird flushes in front of you and flies straight ahead, you can hold right on the bird. Naturally, if that same bird drops or rises, or turns right or left, you will have to compensate.

Some shots will be at overhead, incoming birds, as well, in which event the gunner must shoot ahead of the target. Momentarily the gun barrel may obscure the bird. But the lead, if correct, will pattern nicely.

It is a fact, too, that the gunner need not have to be lightning fast to bag birds on the wing. Any of the upland varieties will flush speedily with a loud burst of wings. The beginner, and even many a trained upland gunner for that matter, will be taken aback by this uproar. Such noise is disconcerting, but try to brush it aside. School yourself to forget it.

Concentrate instead on putting the muzzle ahead of the target, if necessary, and letting the game fly right into the shot charge. Just aim at a spot in front of the bird. Be fast on the upswing, but at the same time deliberate. Don't let the bird fluster you. Point ahead, and when the lead looks right, press the trigger and watch the bird fold.

The hunter who is schooled in taking birds on the wing can

The How-To of Wing Shooting

In a shower of feathers,
a ring-necked pheasant
succumbs to the
unhurried shot of an
experienced wing
shooter and his classic
double. Photo: Leonard
Lee Rue III.

THE SHOTGUN

raise his gun on the rising bird, bag it, and then swing to another without undue exertion, and take that one, too.

The fundamentals of good wing shooting are correct gun position, proper stance, and the right use of lead and swing. Stand squarely on both feet when you shoot. Your weight should be on the forward foot, and when you shoot, pivot from the waist and follow through with the gun moving. When ready to shoot, get your head down, cheek the stock firmly, and keep your cheek there all the time you shoot. With practice this becomes automatic.

It is also important to get out into the field and shoot as much as you can. The more experiences you run into when trying to bag your birds, the more expertise you will have to fall back on. Each shot is a challenge; try to figure it out quickly. With most upland quarry it is a case of now or never.

There is, however, no need to break out in a sweat on a difficult shot. Make up your mind to hit and the chances are you will. There are certain secrets to success and one of the most important is to keep your shots within effective gun range. Another is always to shoot. If you find that you are consistently missing, you may be trying shots beyond the range of your gun. Or your lead may be off.

Trial-and-error is an excellent teacher. Many hunters shoot too fast when the bird flushes. Get the gun up fast at the flush . . . but then take your time.

The How-To of Wing Shooting

4

The Unsurpassed Ruffed Grouse

There is something about ruffed grouse hunting that really sets it apart. It's a superb sport that seems to attract only the cream of hunters each fall, and with just reason. These native birds are amazingly elusive and require a lot of hunting. A man who has taken his full bag has already made his mark as a hunter and wing shot.

The ruffed grouse (*Bonasa umbellus*), also known as the drumming grouse, partridge, mountain pheasant, shoulderknot grouse, white flesher, and wood grouse, is an unpredictable bird. A grouse will never do the expected—what you want it to. It takes a headlong flight when flushed, literally throwing itself into the air, and nearly always manages to put a tree between itself and the gunner.

This was not always so, for at one time the ruffed grouse was a trusting bird and easily taken. The Indians bagged grouse with traps and snares, as well as bows and arrows, and with little trouble. The market gunner took an enormous toll of this bird, with many Eastern markets buying thousands of them for as much as 50 or 75 cents a pair.

In certain remote sections, particularly the Canadian wilderness, the ruffed grouse is still easy to bag, having little fear of man. It is a simple matter to shoot a ruffed grouse out of a tree with a .22. The shooter can start at the bottom branch and work upward, picking off the lower birds first. The shooting seldom bothers the upper birds.

The ruffed grouse is a handsome, beautifully marked bird. About the size of a small chicken, it is one of the largest of the upland-bird clan, measuring some 18 inches in length and weighing 1½ to 2 pounds. Its meat is white and it has a full breast, rather plump for so small a bird.

This is our only grouse with a conspicuous black tailband. The bird shows variations in color from one region to another, but in general the upper parts are brown to dark brown, touched elsewhere with black, gray, and white. Some grouse show a pronounced silver tip in color, while others go through a dark-brown and furous color phase, with little or no gray on the body.

At one time, ruffed grouse would sit on a limb, as shown here, and allow a hunter to walk right up and bash it with a club. Now, the bird may well be the smartest and spookiest game bird of them all. Photo: Leonard Lee Rue III.

The Unsurpassed Ruffed Grouse

The male has a crest that shows clearly when he is startled, as well as the pronounced ruff that gives the bird its name. The female lacks the crest and is duller in color. The ruff, although present in the female, is usually much smaller than the male's, so much so it may be virtually unnoticeable. Both male and female have a wide fan-shaped tail. The tail helps guide them in their erratic flight. The tail feathers have a distinct black band when the tail is fanned open. The voice of the grouse, a nervous *quit-quit,* often reveals its presence to the quietly approaching hunter.

The grouse is a bird of forest and woodland, its plumage blending with the surroundings to a remarkable degree. A nonmigratory bird, the ruffed grouse will be found in the same locality from year to year and is able to withstand even the coldest of winters. With snow on the ground, it will often spend the night buried under a blanket of snow.

For really good grouse hunting, try traveling brushy logging roads and back-country lanes with considerable shade, especially if they offer openings laced with dense grass and weeds. Here and there you may find side roads or trails that provide cover and forage for the birds. In fact, where trails converge on each other you may discover exceptional hunting, for the grouse must have a certain amount of clearance to take off in flight. With a good dog to flush the birds, such roads and trails can provide superlative hunting.

Cutover areas are favored, especially where berries abound. Being omnivorous, the grouse will feed, along with berries, on buds of apple, birch, aspen, and hemlock trees, on tag alder, chokeberry, and cranberry. Its food is roughly 90 percent vegetable and 10 percent insect. Find country where there is plenty of food and cover and chances are grouse will be there. By the same token, rarely is a ruffed grouse found in a spot that does not offer it cover. During the heat of the day it may take a dust bath in the road, but even so there will be foliage or tall grass just a few feet away.

The grouse is not a bird of dense woods, but rather is a

margin or edge-of-the-woods bird, just as is the whitetail deer. In fact, grouse and deer will be found in much the same habitat. Walk along slowly and look and listen. When you approach too close for comfort, your grouse will flush to one side or the other. When grouse are scarce and hard to find, scout the old trails with much grass and brush. Here they may be right in the middle or to the side of the trail, and ever ready to take off. If a fallen tree crosses the trail, be doubly alert, for coveys like such camouflage.

27

Hunting pressure has a lot to do with grouse behavior and the cover they inhabit. With a day or two of much shooting, the birds head for the brush. They hang tight to the edge of the

Tracks of the ruffed grouse in snow. Such tracks will often be found in the vicinity of deer tracks, as the two species favor the same type of terrain. Photo: Leonard Lee Rue III.

trails and are on the alert. The answer is that for shooting you will have to move very quietly and be ready on the instant for the always noisy rise of a bird.

With so many things working against it, the ruffed grouse has to be tricky to survive. Living as it does not far from human habitation, it is hunted long and hard when the season is on, and suffers during the nesting season from such natural predators as raccoon, opossum, skunk, red squirrel, and chipmunk, and later from such enemies as hawk, owl, and fox.

Ruffed grouse, particularly in the North, are cyclic in their population. The cycles occur regularly. There are times when the birds build up in numbers and can be seen in almost every suitable cover. But then they fall into decline, and for several years their population is low, sometimes almost disappearing completely.

When the birds are young, cold and wet weather can have a devastating effect upon them. A cold, wet spring will kill off many grouse chicks by chilling them. Grouse have soft feathers that cannot withstand much wetness. Even adult birds dislike too much moisture, and during a rain will head for the protection of such cover as heavy evergreens.

If this bird were dubbed "His Contrariness, the Ruffed Grouse," it would be aptly named, for it has tricks that hold it in good stead no matter what the circumstances. Sometimes you can go out in the woods and find grouse in considerable numbers. On other days and in the same coverts, you will be lucky if you run into one or two, no matter how hard you hunt.

Morning is the witching hour for grouse hunting. The bird is busy at this time stoking its stomach. It drops down from its tree perch at dawn and feeds for some time. It will be around most of the day, too. But from about noon until three o'clock, it takes its ease, and then usually begins to feed again. The latter feeding provides another time for good hunting. Generally, at the arrival of evening, the grouse flies for its night shelter in the evergreens, where it takes a tight perch close to the trunk until morning.

In the spring, ruffed grouse may be found feeding on budding apple trees. Mark their habits then, and when hunting season comes you'll have a pretty fair idea where to look for them. Photo: Leonard Lee Rue III.

The Unsurpassed Ruffed Grouse

Grouse Range

The range of this bird is wide and varied, running all the way from Alaska down the West Coast, through the Midwest and the Great Lakes States into northern Canada, to the East Coast, and south right into the hill country of Georgia. The heaviest population is along the West Coast, through the Great Lakes region, and into the New England States and the Canadian Maritime Provinces.

Along with the ruffed grouse as we generally know it, there is the Canada ruffed grouse; the Nova Scotia variety; the gray ruffed grouse found chiefly in the Rocky Mountains and into Alaska and east to Manitoba; the Oregon ruffed grouse found in northern California, Oregon, Washington, and British Columbia; and the Yukon ruffed grouse, found in the Yukon Territory and the largest of the ruffed grouse. These grouse vary little in their markings, being essentially much the same as the eastern grouse.

Wherever you find him, the ruffed grouse is a fine game bird—one of the trickiest.

Grouse Guns

There is a difference of opinion about the best gauge for grouse shooting. Many believe that the 20-gauge shotgun is the best and sportiest. But the gauge is largely irrelevant. The 12, 16, or 20 will do fine. Grouse guns, however, should be light and have open chokes of improved cylinder and never more than modified.

The pump is still probably the most often-used shotgun type by grouse hunters. However, there are many who feel that a double barrel is best of all. It is short and handy because it lacks the receiver that houses the action. Over-and-under shotguns, bored improved cylinder and modified, have become popular among grouse hunters in recent years, and their popularity is growing.

5

Hunting
the Western Grouse

One of the problems with hitting sharptails as well as prairie chickens is getting sufficiently close, and then using a gun with a full choke. Most shots are long, and there will be a thunder of wings that tends to unnerve the shooter when the flock arises.

Both sharptails and chickens are species of prairie grouse. They have similar family traits and are hunted pretty much the same. They gather about in flocks, and even when feeding one bird always seems to act as a sentry. Both are birds of the prairies and grasslands, with the sharptail ranging farther north. Both are found in the same type of habitat, however, with similar feeding and flight habits. Both species are large birds, weighing up to 2½ pounds. Where at all in evidence, they are much sought after by the upland gunner because both species are elusive, hard to hit, and especially hard to approach.

The sage grouse is the largest of our grouse. It, too, is a Western bird, inhabiting the sagebrush plains of the West.

The blue grouse is a bird of the Western woodlands. In summer and fall, blue grouse live in mixed open forests. Along the Pacific Coast, it is a popular game bird among upland hunters. It is almost as popular among Western hunters as ruffed grouse among Easterners.

The Sharp-tailed Grouse

Sharptails and chickens are quite different in appearance. The sharp-tailed grouse is the lighter of the two in color.

With the short, pointed tail from which it gets its name pointed straight up and its wings outspread, a male sharptail prepares to go into the quick, stamping dance it uses to attract the female. Photo: Charles G. Summers Jr., % Leonard Rue Enterprises.

Generally it is light gray and brown, with wing feathers liberally dotted with white marks. Its breast and flanks are very light. What also differentiates it from the prairie chicken is its distinctive tail, made up of long, spikelike feathers, with the middle tail feathers extending some distance beyond the rest. The sharptail has often been called the pintail for this reason. Other common names are blackfoot, spiketail, white-bellied grouse, white belly, white grouse, and willow grouse. Its scientific name is *Pedioecetes phasianellus*.

The sharptail is our only grouse with a short, pointed tail. Its flight is fast, straight, and with rapid wingbeats alternating with glides on down-curved wings—quite different from its cousin the ruffed grouse.

A female sharptail in the prairie grass. When hunting, it is virtually impossible to differentiate a female sharptail from a male and in season both can be taken legally. Photo: Charles G. Summers, Jr. % Leonard Rue Enterprises.

Its habitat is open woodlands and grassy prairie lands, and its numbers have risen where grasslands have increased, notably in Canada. Hunting in these areas can be excellent.

The Prairie Chicken

The prairie chicken (*Tympanuchus cupido*) is a predominantly dark bird, with dusky flanks and underparts, and with breast and belly marked with transverse bars like those of the Plymouth Rock chicken. The prairie chicken's tail is short, rounded, and marked by dark tail feathers. The bird on the whole is as sleek looking as its cousin the sharptail. Unlike the ruffed grouse, neither the prairie chicken nor the sharptail has a noticeable chest. The prairie chicken is also known as the pinnated grouse, prairie grouse, squaretail, and yellowlegs.

Male prairie chickens engaging in a territorial dispute. In spring, during the breeding season, each male stakes out his own area for dancing and booming. Any intruder who steps over the invisible line that marks the area is attacked instantly. Photo: Leonard Lee Rue III.

THE SHOTGUN

A male prairie chicken as he looks when not on display. His pinnae, the appendages that stand erect behind his head when he is booming, are here hanging down, covering the deflated air sacs. Photo: Leonard Lee Rue III.

An adult male prairie chicken booming. When he expels the air from the twin sacs on either side of his neck, the prairie chicken produces a loud booming effect that reverberates across the prairie. Photo: Leonard Lee Rue III.

Hunting the Western Grouse

The Sage Grouse

In appearance, the sage grouse (Centrocercus urophasianus) is a large and spectacular bird. The cocks weigh up to 8 pounds, while the hens average over 4 in weight. The bird's color is predominantly ash gray, variegated with black, brown, and whitish yellow. The breast and belly are yellowish gray except for a black patch on the abdomen. In the cock, the tail is very striking. It consists of about twenty long, narrow, pointed feathers which the cock spreads into a striking fan during courtship. The hen is very similar to the cock except that she has much shorter and narrower tail feathers.

Sage grouse depend almost entirely on sagebrush for their livelihood. In winter, sage leaves form an exclusive diet. In spring, the big birds nest in sage; in summer the sagebrush forms ideal cover for young broods. For this reason, the sage grouse is not as abundant as it used to be. Ranchers and farmers have converted vast acres of sage into grass and alfalfa for cattle pasture.

The Blue Grouse

The blue grouse (Dendragapus obscurus) is a large bird, larger than the prairie grouse and the ruffed grouse. Cocks will occasionally tip the scales at 3 pounds or even a shade over. In color, the upper part of the cock bird, including the head and neck, is a grayish black with transverse lines of bluish gray.

The underparts, including the breast, are pale blue-gray becoming lighter toward the back. The tail consists of twenty broad feathers, dusky brown in color with ash-gray marblings. Each tail feather ends with a wide band of light gray. The hen is similar in color to the cock. However, her crown, breast, and sides tend to be marked with a bit more brown.

The range of the blue grouse overlaps that of the ruffed grouse, but each bird exhibits different habitat preferences. The blue grouse prefers more open woodlands than the ruffed grouse. It also has a preference for drier areas, favoring old burns, cutovers, openings near roads, and edges of mountain meadows. These are the areas where wild fruits and berries, green shoots, and buds are most abundant, and that's where blue grouse should be hunted.

Hunting Methods

Sharptails and prairie chickens are so alike that the methods of hunting them are practically the same. Since they take to the open woodlands and prairie stretches, they can be hunted with dogs. Shots are usually on the long side, and one of the big problems is to approach close enough for shooting action.

There are still a few northern plains states where prairie grouse can be hunted. The sand hills country of Nebraska is one of the best places for sharptails. But sharptails are found from Colorado northward to Alaska, and from there eastward through Alberta, Saskatchewan, and the Dakotas, through Minnesota, Wisconsin, and even northern Ontario.

The prairie chicken has a much more restricted range. It is found from South Dakota westward to Nebraska and Kansas, and south to Oklahoma, Texas, and New Mexico.

Some of the best gunning can be had in the Dakotas from early October until the end of November. During the opening days the grouse are hunted zealously. But later in the season the pressure is down, making this a propitious time for getting in some productive gunning. Certainly many of the natives in the know take advantage of this lull and enjoy much late-season grouse hunting. At this time the birds gather in larger coveys.

In South Dakota, sharptails and chickens are frequently

found in the same cover. As long as the season is open on both species, one can take either or both as he sees fit, within legal limits, of course. Locating the birds early in the season is not much of a trick, as they seem to favor the shelter of berry bushes and grassy spots in the valleys where it is warn and the forage is plentiful.

Later in the season the big birds leave these more sheltered confines and take to the wider prairie stretches and vast corn-fields. Here they can successfully be hunted by groups of sportsmen making a drive. Frequently the birds will also take shelter in the long grass and weeds that hide them well, and are best found and flushed with well-trained dogs of the point-ing type.

When the hunting is at its peak, flocks of prairie grouse will fly into the cornfields. If the hunter can wangle permission to hunt there, he will find that the birds come in to feed either just at dawn or toward midafternoon. The birds have regular feed-ing areas and visit these daily. The trick is to remain hidden as the birds sail in.

The sage grouse is not our most sporting bird to hunt. It is just not a fast flier. The sport comes in finding it.

The sage grouse is something of a vagabond. The season generally opens early—late August in some states. By then the broods of sage grouse generally begin to migrate higher up the ridges and slopes. The places to look for these big grouse are in large stands of sage, but not far from green fields of hay and alfalfa, particularly if they are enhanced by streams.

It's a mistake at this time to hunt the vast sage-covered plains. It's best to stick to the edges, because in summer the birds like to feed on green grasses and other green shoots. The birds feed more heavily in the mornings and late afternoons. During midday, they tend to dust and loaf under shade.

Some states have October and even November sage-grouse seasons. By then, the birds are found higher on the sage-covered hillsides where they will spend the winter. Fall is the time to hunt sage grouse in the sage.

The hen sage grouse is much harder to hit than the cock. Hens are smaller for one thing. They flush more rapidly and fly faster. They also twist from side to side in flight. This is true for young sage grouse of either sex as well. Old cocks are rather slow to rise and they fly low and straight.

Dogs can be very useful for sage-grouse hunting, because a dog can cover wide areas. This is where a wide-ranging dog proves his superiority. Some pointing dogs trained to hunt grouse, quail, and pheasant may not point the strange-smelling sage grouse right from the start. But they soon learn. Certainly sage grouse hold well for a dog. And crippled birds can be hard to find in the thick cover of sage without a dog.

The best state for sage-grouse hunting is Wyoming. But Colorado is also good, as are parts of Utah, Montana, and Idaho. Sage grouse can also be found in California, eastern Oregon and Washington, and southern Alberta.

The blue grouse, like its cousin the ruffed grouse, is a game bird with a split personality. In wilderness areas, the blue grouse is a naive bird, not-at-all afraid of man. But in areas where people, particularly hunters, are common, the blue grouse can be almost as wary as the ruffed grouse.

The blue grouse flushes with the same thunderous wingbeat as the ruffed grouse and flies around trees with equal skill. And since the bird frequently flies downhill, its flight is even faster than that of a ruffed grouse. A blue grouse hurling itself down a mountain side is no easy target.

Blue grouse are migratory birds, moving down the mountain slopes in spring and back up the slopes in fall. The old cocks migrate down first to take up breeding territories, and again migrate first into wintering habitat.

During early fall, the birds should be hunted in open forests near grassy clearings. At times, aspen groves will hold birds. If in early fall you are finding only hens and young of the year, it means that the old cock birds have already migrated into the fir forests higher up the mountains.

For best results, hunting should be concentrated in areas

Hunting the Western Grouse

which have an abundance of berry- and fruit-producing shrubs and trees, along with water. Blue grouse can frequently be found close to mountain streams and rills. Equally good are small springs and seepages which have green grass nearby. Blue grouse, like ruffed grouse, favor greens once in a while. The hunter should avoid vast, dense stands of evergreen, because little food for grouse exists there. But the edges of evergreen stands can be very good. Blue grouse frequently roost in coniferous trees.

Blue grouse tend to do most of their feeding during midmorning and midafternoon. They generally wait to feed until the dew has dried off. When the birds are feeding, they are much easier to find than when they are loafing somewhere in thick cover. Dogs have an easier time locating grouse when they are feeding because the birds leave more scent then.

Any dog that can handle ruffed grouse can also handle blues. In fact, blues are probably a little easier for dogs. Flushing dogs and pointing dogs can be used equally well.

The best places to hunt blue grouse are remote areas. Blue grouse hunters need stout legs to walk the hillsides. A four-wheel-drive rig or a horse is very useful in getting the hunter into remote blue-grouse country.

In wilderness areas, blue-grouse hunting does not represent much sport. But then the trappers, Indians, and big-game hunters that penetrate the wilderness don't hunt blue grouse for sport. They take the bird for the pot, and they seldom even use a shotgun. They prefer instead a .22 rimfire rifle or even a handgun. Big-game hunters even occasionally hand-load small-game loads for their big-game rifles, so that they can take grouse for the pot.

Guns and Loads

The birds may be taken a bit closer in the cornfields than in the grasslands, but even so the gun should ideally be a

12 gauge patterned so that it throws enough pellets to kill birds at a good 35 to 40 yards. Larger shot sizes are recommended for this type of shooting—especially No. 6s, but some hunters even prefer 4s.

If the double-barreled shotgun is used, full and modified chokes are most practical. When using the single barrel, a full choke is your best choice unless you install a variable choke.

The best gun for sage grouse is a 12 gauge with a full-choke barrel. But in summer, a modified choke may be better because the birds usually hold tighter. In a pinch, a hunter could use one of the smaller gauges—16 or 20—but the 12 is best.

The reason for selecting a 12 is that the birds are shot at longer ranges and they're tough. It takes a good, dense pattern of coarse shot to bring them down. This is why No. 4 shot is best as well. The best loads are magnums with 1½ ounces of shot.

The 12 gauge is also the most popular for blue grouse, but the 20 and 16 are fairly effective. Western hunters tend to lean toward the pump and semiauto.

There is probably no ideal choke. Early in the season an improved cylinder is better because the birds generally hold better. But a modified is also useful because longer shots are possible in the open woodlands where blue grouse are hunted. A hunter using a pointing dog will be better off with an improved cylinder, while a hunter with a flushing dog might want a modified choke because of the longer ranges.

Since blue-grouse hunting ideally calls for both improved cylinder and modified chokes, a double-barreled shotgun—whether side-by-side or over-under—is probably the best choice.

The best shot size is also in dispute. Some hunters prefer 7½s early in the season and switch to 6s later on, while others swear by 6s at all times.

Hunting the Western Grouse

6

Mystery Migrant of the Uplands— The Woodcock

Here one day and gone the next—that is the woodcock (*Philohela minor*), the mystery bird of the uplands. Not exactly spectacular in its daily life, it is nonetheless a thrilling bird to hunt, especially as it springs from the grass with a startled whistling in its wings. Woodcock hunting is a game in itself. During the months of September and October, when the flight is on, the sport is at its headiest. And the scenery is magnificent wherever the bird is found.

I still remember my first woodcock. The long-billed bird rose very close. Recognizing it in the air, I shot and luckily missed. Had I hit at such close range, the bird would have been mangled. With my second shot, I managed to pick it off and the bird retained that delicate mixture of plumage and beauty that is distinctly its own. It made a nice addition to the game bag.

The woodcock is a unique bird. Neither a true upland inhabitant nor a shore bird, it is a link between the two. It belongs to the snipe family and is a close relative of the sandpipers, godwits, and curlews of the family Scolopacidae. Not large, it does weigh a bit more than the jacksnipe. It has a tendency to a protuberant belly and a well-fed look, and in size is about on a par with a quail.

In coloration the woodcock is truly handsome, its back feathers beautiful in woodland browns touched with black and buff markings. In general the bird is brown and black with a short tail and a long, slender bill. Soft and fluffy, its breast is a creamy buff. The stubby tail is marked with black and white. Very alert, dark, and prominent eyes are set high and protrude. The eyes are encircled with a narrow line of white.

43

Many common names have been given to this bird, among them big eyes, big-eyed john, big mudsnipe, bogsucker, briar snipe, hill partridge, timberdoodle, Labrador twister, little whistler, night flit, night peck, swamp partridge, whistling snipe, woodhen, and woodsnipe. In fact, the woodcock seems to have a different name in each locality where it's found.

Bad weather is the woodcock's greatest enemy. Cold, wet springs kill many chicks, which hatch earlier than most other game birds. Late snows and frosts also take their toll of adults, depriving them of food. Other than that, some woodcock are taken by a variety of predators, but predation is not considered to be a limiting factor to woodcock populations.

Early in the fall, woodcock tend to head for winter quarters, many inhabiting the bottomlands of Louisiana. Moonlight nights are favored for these prolonged flights, usually in October. The birds land temporarily, year after year, in about the same places. Their grounds must be on the wet side, for 85 percent of the woodcock's diet is earthworms, which it seeks in low, wooded bottomlands. Low trees and dense foliage shadow the covert, and the bird, when found, is usually on the ground and feeding. Woodcock must select cover with plenty of food, for they are prodigious eaters. The hunter should look for earthworm borings, a sure sign of the bird, along with a whitewash of droppings.

Mystery Migrant of the Uplands–The Woodcock

In locating woodcock, head for low-brushed hillsides and deserted farmlands with apple orchards and sapling growths of alder, sycamore, and willow. You will also often find the bird in tag alder swamps as well as higher up in pine, poplar, and birch stands. The small poplar trees retain their leaves until late in the fall and provide fine hiding and feeding possibilities for woodcock.

If you can discover an old orchard in sparsely settled hunting fields, you may also run into woodcock, since these places produce a good crop of worms. You will also run into woodcock among bracken ferns and briar thickets. Avoid mossy grounds. These are void of earthworms. Nor do woodcock care for cultivated fields, stands of high grass, or heavily wooded lands. Just where you will pinpoint the bird at a certain time is not always predictable. Woodcock seem to have their own notions as to where they want to be at any time. They are secretive, largely nocturnal, and solitary. Normally they take to flight around dusk to feed, and then again at dawn when they head for their resting grounds. These places are usually no more than a mile apart.

The woodcock tends to sit tight until you are almost on it. Even then it might not flush. Without a dog, the hunter is liable to pass up many birds. But with a dog, you will cover much more territory and secure twice as much shooting.

The best dog is a pointing dog, one that keeps the bird locked up until you walk in for the shot. If the dog can be taught to retrieve, so much the better. The woodcock is small and may be hard to find in the tangle it usually inhabits. There is something about the odor of woodcock, however, that offends the noses of some dogs. Some may refuse to retrieve the downed quarry.

Another dog of value on woodcock is the spaniel. The spaniel may cover himself with briars and burrs in the course of the hunt, but if trained on woodcock, he will add zest to the hunt and kick out a good percentage of the woodcock on the premises.

THE SHOTGUN

Good woodcock hunting lies in the Great Lakes States and in New England, but the mecca for many woodcockers is New Brunswick. During the winter months, Louisiana offers some top woodcock shooting. However, many Southern hunters don't take full advantage of it.

The long, slender bill of the portly, somewhat ungainly woodcock is handy for drilling holes in the ground in the bird's endless search for the earthworms on which it feeds. Photo: Michigan Conservation Department.

Woodcock depend largely upon their natural camouflage for safety and often show a disinclination to flush. A dog can make all the difference in hunting them, even though many dogs will refuse to retrieve woodcock. Photo: Leonard Lee Rue III.

Guns and Loads for Woodcock

A short-barreled, open-choked 20-gauge double with No. 7½ or 8 chilled shot makes an excellent choice for this small bird, as it can also be used on any grouse you happen upon. Mount the gun quickly and then wait for the woodcock to straighten out at the top of its corkscrew rise. Find it over the top of the barrel as it levels off and hope for the best.

If it's amiss, follow the flight of the bird and try for another shot. Chances are the woodcock may settle down not more than 50 yards away, for it is a fast but not a far flyer. The snap shot, bringing the gun up quickly but smoothly, is the recommended procedure. Woodcock do not emulate the nerve-racking and twisting rise of the ruffed grouse, but will be fast and swerving, providing a small target ahead of the gun.

Hints for Success

Avoid dressing too warmly when going after wood-cock. The weather may be cool, but the cover will mostly be dense with little wind. Your jacket and breeches should be of hard-fabric material to withstand switchy cover, and your boots watertight hunting pacs. A light woolen shirt is ideal at this time of year.

The best time for action is early in the morning, when the woodcock is still on its postnocturnal feeding binge. If the flight is in you will find the birds close together, and when you flush and shoot one bird, another might flush close by. So be ready.

Flight Birds and Local Birds

The woodcock is migratory. Just about the time you find birds and get some fast and tricky shooting, the birds will be on their way. That is the time the frost has stripped the foliage from the trees and the snow is beginning to fall. The birds at this time have trouble finding food and are on their way south.

Watch for flight birds late in the season. They come in from the north and may tarry for a time. The snow may melt, and the flight birds may arrive overnight and stick around. But depend primarily on local birds for your shooting; it may be spotty, but it will be more reliable.

Local birds are found principally in Pennsylvania, Wisconsin, Michigan, New York, New Jersey, and the New England States. In such places the local woodcock will bring up their young in sheltered spots along streams and rivers, and although the locals are not as numerous as the flight birds, they will be present when the season opens.

Listen for the whine of wings in heavy cover. Listening to the bird take off, you know that it will not go far. This makes close hunting a real game and a fine chance to pick up a bird here and there, or at least a possibility of marking the lie of the woodcock. It can be extremely close, so be ready for a quick shot.

In heavy alders and poplar I have kept busy for several hours flushing bird after bird. The woodcock alight, heaven only knows exactly where, and you go in for them with anticipation. If they flush almost in your face, don't be too surprised. The bird itself is so small, with a lot of plumage to fill it out, that small shot is called for, with a low powder charge to send it along. The small shot will make for a denser shot pattern, with more pellets going to the mark than when using large shot sizes. At the same time, with the birds taking off through so many twigs and branches, some percentage of this shot charge is stopped before it reaches the bird. The gunner must use a larger number of pellets in the load for a killing pattern on his game.

Mystery Migrant of the Uplands–The Woodcock

7

Hunting
the Gaudy Ringneck

You can never be sure about pheasants. They often look like easy marks, but until they're securely tucked away in your game bag they're anything but. One thing you'll find out for sure is that you'll have to kill the bird cleanly or it will scuttle away in the brush.

Get out early and hunt. In the first part of the season, the prime hunting is in cornfields and edges of grain stubbles—places where the birds are well fed and feel right at home. For a time, that is. Once the season is on in earnest, it doesn't take the birds long to discover their vulnerability. From then on they're more elusive. They still do head for the fields early where the pickings are good, but having eaten, they will quickly repair to weedy hideouts to digest. The ringneck will eat as much as its crop will hold, then leave. To get enough grain may take only a half hour or so, but it will require several hours to digest. The bird will spend the rest of the day digesting what it has and picking up other edibles in as secure a hideout as possible. This somewhat concealed resting area will not be far from its favorite grainfield, so find such a place to hunt when the feeding grounds are vacated.

A ringneck's liking for corn especially will sometimes take it to the vicinity of humans and farm buildings during the first part of the season. But this bird will also eat any grain that is available, and this it will often find on the outskirts of cultivated land. Other preferred foods are insects, seeds, fruits, and berries. The pheasant must have water to survive, also, and will prefer cover that is near a permanent source of it. This is something to remember when the weather is dry.

Once a native of the plains of Asia and Asia Minor and introduced into the United States in 1881, the ring-necked pheasant, *Phasianus colchicus,* is certainly here to stay. Sharp, tricky, wily, and crafty, the pheasant, commonly called the Chinese ringneck but really a distinct American variety now, has endeared itself to thousands of upland gunners. There are others, however, who object to its proclivity for driving other game birds off any range it decides to inhabit.

With both man and natural predators on its trail, in season and out, the pheasant has to fight to survive. But this bird is hardy. The ringneck may not exactly relish forested regions with much snow and cold, but given an agricultural background with no such extremes, the pheasant will move in and multiply.

Certain tricks of survival characterize the ringneck. For instance, where most upland birds take to wing when flushed, the pheasant frequently prefers to leg it along the ground. This is one reason it takes to weedy cover when the hunting pressure is heavy.

Hiding in weeds often occurs late in the season. For example, there was the time we were hunting rabbits on a cold November day, using a beagle to rouse the game. We sent the little dog into one ragweed field in which we were pretty sure a cottontail or two was hiding. As we followed well in back of

Hunting the Gaudy Ringneck

the little hound, we caught sight of a bright flash of pheasant feathers.

Halfway down the field the beagle caught the scent of the ringneck. He came along slowly, a bit bewildered, until he almost ran into the crafty bird. If the pheasant had taken to the air it would have been a dead shot either for my partner or me. Instead, the big bird scuttled across the field with the dog close behind, and finally hit the air, cackling loudly, too far away for a shot. Much pheasant cover is of this sort—heavy stuff, marked by tunnelways cut through the brush and weeds. The birds will use these escape routes wherever possible.

The male ringneck is a colorful and exotic-looking bird, with brilliant plumage and a stunning, long tail that streams in the wind as he flies. The ringneck is quite large as game birds go, the male being up to 35 inches long. The head of the rooster is deep black-green, with red wattles and white collar that stands out sharply. The breast is reddish, touched with black, gray, green, and brown. Weight is from 2½ to 3 pounds. The voice is a harsh c-a-a-a-a, reminiscent of an old automobile horn.

In no way can the hen be mistaken for the cock, for she is much dowdier—a blend of buff, mottled with dark brown. The hen is smaller, has a shorter tail than the male, and also rises at a lower and longer angle, with less noise. The hen is protected in most areas.

Much prolific pheasant acreage is found in Iowa, Illinois, South Dakota, Idaho, the southern parts of Minnesota, Michigan, and Wisconsin; as well as almost clear across the northern and central tier of the United States where there is not much snow. For instance, pheasants are numerous in southern Michigan, but are almost entirely absent in the Upper Peninsula, where snowfall is heavy and there is severe cold in the fall and winter. Pheasants also prosper in the East, but do not do well in the South.

Hitting the bird is not always easy. Once in the air, the pheasant skims along and then rises. The ringneck can be hit even here if the shot is not too far, but that shot must be well placed for results. The pheasant has hard feathers, so it's best to aim for the head. Should the bird appear to falter on any shot, fire again. Although seemingly large, the bird is no easy target, unless close, for if it is only slightly winged it will run for some distance before it flushes, if it does so at all.

The best dogs for pheasant hunting are the setters and pointers, although these breeds may not rate too highly as retrievers, an important angle in the game.

Where the cover is dense, a basset or beagle may be used. Another excellent pheasant dog is the Labrador retriever. Strong and willing, the Labrador will keep on the hunt all day, and has a nose for game second to none combined with the ability to hunt rough cover. With his short coat and strong build, he is well able to negotiate the weeds and brush in fine style and come out clean. Moreover, nothing seems to daunt

An outraged ringneck looks like he's about to give the photographer a piece of his mind. Most hunters won't get anywhere near this close to such a bird before he either legs it or flushes. Photo: Michigan Conservation Department

Hunting the Gaudy Ringneck

A going-away shot at a departing pheasant. Timing is of the essence here; hurry the shot and you're apt to miss, tarry and the bird might well get out of range. Photo: Leonard Lee Rue III.

this dog. In fact, it may prove to be overzealous. But many gun dog authorities rate the springer spaniel as the best pheasant dog ever. There is no doubt that a springer hunts with a vigor and zest that no Lab can match.

Group Hunting

Pheasant hunting can be excellent sport for a group of hunters. Starting out at some logical point in the field, the party might spread out and fan across the cover. With a few men at the other end of the pheasant hideout, the main body deploys in a pretty straight line and takes the birds as they rise before them.

A hen pheasant takes wing. Although protected for the most part, in some regions and in some years hens are legal game. As game biologist John Madson has pointed out, however, the practice is risky, as "hens have enough grief with blizzards and haymowers without being gunned in the bargain." Photo: Leonard Lee Rue III.

Wise in the way of pheasants, Bob Elman holds up a brace of males taken with his 12-gauge Winchester Model 101 over/under. Photo: Leonard Lee Rue III.

When pushed, some birds will usually take wing and offer many and varied shots to the drivers, as well as to those posted at the fringe of the field. The cover may be combed several times with profit, for not always do the birds flush when first alarmed. At the end of the driven field the birds go up in numbers, if there.

At such times the sport is heady and pleasant, and often much game is bagged. There is no guarantee of it, however, unless the field is well chosen and the hunters are cool and expert game shots. The opening days of this party sport are usually marked by much shooting and many birds taken.

Even so, the lone hunter can get in his licks, either at the onset of the season or later, if he is persistent. The best course for the unaccompanied gunner is to trek through the cover, facing the wind, keeping both eyes and ears open for possible targets. Always try to drive the birds out of deep cover toward a clearing where they are more likely to take wing and afford you a shot or two. Birds will usually be left even after some days of intensive hunting. Morning hours are best. The preferred gun is a 12 or 16 gauge, modified choke, although many hunters make a bag with the 20. The best shot is No. 6 in heavy field loads.

8

The American Quail

If there is one upland bird that fits into the American scene to perfection it is the bobwhite quail, *Colinus virginianus*. Not a large bird, not as swift as some nor as tricky, the bobwhite has nonetheless endeared itself to thousands of upland gunners as the only bird that is "fit to hunt."

Popular, ubiquitous, and really a covey bird, the bobwhite is legal for hunting in more states than any other upland game bird. Better than thirty states have open season on it.

Appearance and Distribution

The bobwhite is rather small, being about 10 inches in size. It is plump, rotund, and has sturdy legs and feet. Its bill is short and decurved. Its general colors are a softly mottled brown-and-black, with whitish throat and a breast marked with several shades of brown and white. The bobwhite has a whitish coloring around the eye, especially noticeable in the male. Its tail is short and dark. Its voice is a clear whistled *bobwhite*, and the covey call is *quoi-lee*.

Locating good quail country is essential. As bobwhites are predominantly seed eaters, the country they prefer will usually be farming land, especially old-fashioned farming land with hedgerows and fenceline weeds. When the hunt is on, consider that the birds leave their roosts at dawn but do not go far to feed until about midmorning, at which time they feed extensively and then head back into the thickets after noon for a rest period. Hunt during midmorning as much as possible; then keep the dogs in check and head out once more toward midafternoon, for that is when the quail will feed heavily again, until they head back for their roosts toward dusk.

Where there's food there will be the potential for quail. You will find good quail habitat and hunting on farms growing corn, soybeans, buckwheat, sorghum, lespedeza, and the like. In this cover hunt the overgrown fencerows for best shooting, as well as brushy vales and ravines and overgrown creek banks. This may be country that should be looked over carefully before the hunting season begins. Terrain such as this in Iowa, Indiana, Ohio, Maryland, Delaware, Tennessee, South Carolina, Florida, Texas, and New Mexico, especially, has provided outstanding quail hunting.

You will do well to wear outdoor clothing that can take rough use, as much quail cover is brushy and you may have to do some extensive hiking at times. Luck may be spotty. Then again you can run into covey after covey in covers that favor the birds, and which they hate to leave.

This bird loves the fencerows where it blends closely with its surroundings. When flushed, it explodes into a low, fast flight, scaling quickly down into cover. Bobwhite will occasionally take to a tree, but they're mostly terrestrial. The flight of this quail is generally inclined to be rather straight, and speed is not their greatest asset.

In the South, especially, the bobwhite has traditionally been the bird. On big plantations, shoots for this bird took on the aspects of a festive event. Invariably dogs were a large and vital part of a Southern quail hunt, along with horse and buggy for transportation to and from quail country, and scouts and helpers to aid in the hunt. To top it off, there was always the makings of a satisfying noon meal included. Changing habitat has diminished the Southern quail population, although there are still plantations where the old traditions are honored.

Habitat

As with so many other upland birds, get to know its habits and habitat and you should find bobwhite. Its favorite coverts are in farmlands where it can feed along the ground on seeds and grain. The bobwhite is also never far from human habitation, which is another trait that endears it to many an American hunter. Discover a place that harbors this familiar bird, hunt it with an able dog, and you're in for a day of active, healthy exercise. Note, however, that bobwhite dislike rainy weather as well as storms of any kind. When the day is inclement the birds will hide, and while you may run into one or

A typical bobwhite quail. It is probable that this species is gone after by more hunters than any other upland game bird. Photo: Leonard Lee Rue III.

two, it is advisable to stay out of the field on such days. Remember, too, that after a rain or a cold spell, quail may not budge as early as they otherwise do.

Quail also dislike windy conditions and bone-dry and dust-laden days. Choose the weather that you prefer to hunt in—pleasant days—and there is every chance the quail will cooperate if they are there.

How to Shoot

To become a consistent shot on quail the hunter must know how to anticipate the flurry of the rise, and then place himself in a spot that will take advantage of the terrain. The terrain is the thing!

Quail will head for cover nine times out of ten when flushed, and to stand between the bevy and this objective is a mistake.

Gambel's quail is found in the deserts of the Southwest, where it feeds on such fare as mesquite seeds. Like other Western quail, this bird would generally prefer to run than to fly. Photo: Len Rue, Jr.

The plumed California, or valley, quail is a West Coast inhabitant. The birds tend to flock together, especially in areas containing seed-bearing weeds, grain, or grapevines. Photo: Len Rue, Jr.

In such an event the quail will beat back over your head and swing around you in a sharp curve, necessitating a difficult, overhead shot at short range.

Study the lie of the birds and stand away from the expected flight. Your shot will then be a straightaway. Now, pick one bird out of the rising flock. At times the quartering angle is often easier than the straightaway, leading by about a foot. Above all, don't hurry. Notice the flight pattern, snap the gun to the proper lead, and close the aim evenly. You want to shoot before the quail reaches cover, but not until it is far enough away—say 20 yards—for your shot load to pattern efficiently.

The bobwhite's coloring is deceptive. At times the bird seems to fade into the natural backdrop. The light and shadow of autumn are kind to the quail, tricky to the gunner. But this is part of the game and adds to the sport.

Guns and Loads for Bobwhite

When you pick out a quail gun, it pays to learn it from A to Z, backward and forward. Handle it; get it up fast. There must be no hesitation or deliberation as to how it will operate or where you will point. Quail wait for nobody. They must be dropped quickly and decisively, with no time for tracking and swinging-through as you would on a bird like the pheasant. For the consistent quail gunner, the weapon should fit and handle easily.

What gun is this? Some time ago the double was the gun. It still is to a certain extent, but in the over-under style rather than the traditional side-by-side. Today, many bobwhite hunters use the pump. Many a good bobwhite shot will choose the 20-gauge pump with 20-inch ventilated-rib barrel and open boring. One reason for preferring the pump to the double is that the former is less costly. I like the pump also because it can be fired more than once or twice without reloading. Your shot is there for at least a covey. All you have to do is fire it, pump in another shell quickly, and fire again.

The American Quail

What gauge? There is no reason why the 12 gauge won't do the job on quail, but the truth is that you'll be lugging around more gun than you need, especially if you spend all day in the field. I suggest the 20 gauge, with the 28 a possibility if you find your birds getting up close and you're an extra-good shot.

Avoid the full choke by all means. For quail, you will come out in good shape using an improved-cylinder boring. With open-choked 20 or 28 pumps you can nail any close bird with the first shot and then have enough shells to get on a second or conceivably a third quail.

The choice of shells for bobwhite hunting should fall into the field-load category with a light powder charge, and in sizes 7½ or 8. Low-base 8s are really effective, giving uniform patterns and power enough to drop your quail then and there.

The quail gun can also be your choice for woodcock and ruffed grouse; one that you take into the field for real sport and successful shooting.

Western Quail

The bobwhite has counterparts in the West—notably the California or valley quail and the beautiful Gambel's, a crested bird of the mesquite and cholla thickets of the desert. Other species are the scaled or blue quail, sometimes called the cottontop quail for this little white-tipped crest, and the mountain quail, the largest of our quails, with a crest made up of several long, straight, upright black feathers.

Of these species, only the California quail lies well to the dog, at times. The others have an inborn fear of anything resembling a coyote, their mortal enemy, and will run rather than fly when a dog appears. So it's best to forget a dog when after the rest of these Western quail, and head out with a partner or partners into reputed quail country. By noting the feathers and droppings, along with tracks in the dust, the hunter can find one bevy after another in thickets, prickly pear, brush, arroyos, and other such quail habitat.

Usually Western quail will run when flushed, and when they do flush will go far before alighting. Hunting in the desert for desert quail may be somewhat easy, but quail hunting in the mountains can be quite the reverse, calling for a lot of legwork and shooting that may be on the long side. For Western quail, then, the 12 gauge, bored improved cylinder or modified, pushing No. 7½ chilled shot is recommended.

The best plan when hunting Western quail is to locate the whereabouts of several large bevies and go after them hard. If signs point to good hunting the gunners can form a party and push the birds out with several chances of a shot. Many times you can locate the birds by listening to their feeding sounds, which are often twittering and musical. In the case of the blue quail, the voice is a nasal, friendly, *pecos, pecos*. In the case of the Gambel's, the sound is a musical *keep, keep* when the birds are about to flush, and a *los papagos, los papagos* when they have strayed and are trying to find each other.

Most of these Western quail are not fast fliers. The exception is the Gambel's, which has bulletlike speed, and taken on the wing must be given a lot of lead. Western quail may make for difficult hunting, but they are exciting targets.

Scaled quail, another desert bird, is probably the fastest runner of the quails. Some frustrated hunters take their shots at the running birds, a practice most wing shooters deplore, but that is probably not too much different from shooting desert jackrabbits.
Photo: Len Rue, Jr.

9

Gunning for
Huns and Chukars

Like the ring-necked pheasant, the Hungarian and chukar partridges are recent immigrants to our shores. And like the pheasant, huns and chukars have made themselves right at home. Upland hunters can be thankful, because both huns and chukars live in an environment that frequently cannot support any of our native game birds. On top of this, both are first-class game.

The Hungarian Partridge

The Hungarian partridge *(Perdix perdix)* is a true partridge, whereas the ruffed grouse, sometimes colloquially also called the partridge, is a grouse.

The Hungarian partridge is also a handsome bird, with a quail-like shape but twice the size. The overall coloring of the hun is a gray-brown. The breast is gray and the males frequently have a chestnut abdominal patch. The back and upper parts are chestnut brown, as are the tail feathers. The color of the tail feathers is conspicuous in flight.

The Hungarian partridge should actually be called the gray partridge—the correct English name for the bird. The name gray partridge is certainly more descriptive. The reason we call it the Hungarian partridge is because the early stock of birds on this continent came from Hungary. But in Europe the gray partridge is found from the British Isles and across the whole of the continent to the plains of Russia.

63

The Chukar

Like the hun, the chukar (*Alectoris graeca*) is a true partridge. Its name is not quite as descriptive, however, as it should be. In Europe, the bird is called the red-legged partridge. We get the name of chukar because our first stocks came from the Himalayan Mountains of India. But in the old world, red-legged partridges are found from Holland south into Spain and eastward into India.

In appearance, the chukar is a bluish-gray bird approaching the ruffed grouse in size. The bird's underparts are buff, but the breast is gray. The throat and cheeks are white framed with a band of brownish black. The flanks are boldly marked with black and chestnut. The beak, feet, and legs are red.

Habitat and Range

Although the Hungarian and chukar partridges can share the same habitat in parts of their Western range, the ideal habitat for huns is less arid than that for chukars.

Huns are adaptable birds. They can live from the lush farming country of the East to the dry wheat farms of the West. Huns are predominantly a farming-country game bird, but this doesn't mean that they do not live in nonagricultural lands. It is probable that at one time huns were a bird of the wild grasslands of Europe, but with the coming of agriculture they adapted to the changes in habitat so that the ideal habitat type lies on the fringes of farming areas. The farms must not be too clean, though. They must offer good nesting cover and good cover for growing broods.

The range of huns is highly variable. They are found in wheat-farming areas from eastern Washington and Oregon north to Alberta and Saskatchewan, south into Nevada, across Wyoming, Idaho, and Montana into South Dakota and Iowa, and into Minnesota, Wisconsin, and Illinois.

In the East, there are huns in Canada's Atlantic Provinces of Prince Edward Island, Nova Scotia, and New Brunswick, in the St. Lawrence valley of western Quebec, and in eastern Ontario, even stretching down into New York State. Ohio also has huns.

But the best Hungarian partridge habitat is in the Western states. The birds are fairly winter hardy—much more so than bobwhite or pheasant—so the Western winters don't bother them all that much unless extremely deep snows occur. Part of the reason why huns do not do as well in the East is because of more intensive agriculture; but also, the East has more rain in the spring, which cannot be tolerated by broods of young. In cold, wet springs, many broods die from exposure. Ice storms that glaze over food and cover can also cause havoc among hun coveys in winter.

Chukars have a more restrictive habitat demand than huns. They are birds of arid, hilly country with patches of cheatgrass or ricegrass plus low-lying shrubs such as greasewood, sagebrush, and saltbrush. At times they can also be found on the fringes of grain-growing areas, close to the bottoms of valleys.

When chukars were first introduced to this continent in the 1930s, they were stocked in a variety of places including the rich farming country of the Midwest. The reasoning was that if the birds could survive in dry, inhospitable habitat, they could really do well in rich habitat. It didn't work. The chukars found neither the East nor the Midwest to their liking. But they felt right at home in the arid West.

The reason for this may have been that we obtained our stock from the arid hills of India. Thus the birds were adapted to a dry climate and relatively sparse cover. Had we obtained our stock from Europe, the story might have been different. Actually, I'm just as glad it happened the way it did, because chukars filled an empty niche on this continent. They provide upland-game gunning in areas that are largely unused by any native game bird.

This, of course, does not mean that there is no overlap with other game-bird species. I have already written that chukars and huns overlap. There are hunters in Idaho who have shot both birds out of the same covey. Valley quail, mountain quail, and sage grouse can also be occasionally encountered in chukar country, just as sharp-tailed grouse can sometimes be found during a Hungarian partridge hunt.

The habitat requirements of arid, relatively sparsely covered hills narrows the range of the chukar to the drier portions of the Western hills. Chukars range from southern British Columbia south to Colorado. The Western states that offer chukar hunting include eastern Oregon and Washington, Montana, Wyoming, Idaho, Utah, California, and Nevada. Hawaii also has chukars on its arid hillsides. Many shooting preserves in the East and the Midwest also offer chukar shooting for their clients. The chukar is much easier to rear in captivity than the Hungarian partridge.

Hunting Techniques

In the fall, huns depend heavily on fallen grain left in the stubbles for feed. But they will also feed on a variety of weed seeds, so grain is not indispensable. A hunter must keep this in mind when looking for birds. When feeding on cultivated grains, huns show a preference to wheat and barley over

Gunning for Huns and Chukars

corn or oats. That's another thing a hunter should keep in mind. If the area in which you are hunting has all four grains, hunt the wheat and barley stubbles first.

However, it would be a mistake to hunt huns in the Western states solely in agricultural areas. The birds will also live in rolling foothills covered with grass and sage, quite far from the nearest grain field. There is little doubt in my mind, though, that the best hun hunting is in farming country or around its edges.

Hungarian partridge don't need water. They can live on water from early morning dew and from moisture in green grass. Consequently, hunters don't need to stay near water courses as they would when hunting pheasants. But in many areas, huns share pheasant habitat. This is also true in Europe.

One way to find huns is to ask local farmers and ranchers. But the Hungarian partridge lives an unpublicized life. I have had one farmer tell me he had never seen such birds on his land, but within an hour my dog found five coveys on a 200-acre farm. If farmers and ranchers in hun country tell you there are no huns about, don't necessarily accept their word.

Hunters out gunning for Hungarian partridge must always keep in mind that huns are a covey bird and can run almost like a pheasant. In the early fall, the covey consists of the young and their two parents. The cock Hungarian partridge is monogamous. He stays close to the hen when she is incubating and then helps with the rearing of the family.

In good years with warm, dry springs, a covey of huns will number twelve to sixteen birds. On the ground the covey acts like one bird. All members run and flush in unison. The covey instinct in huns is so strong that even in flight the covey does not scatter to the same extent as a covey of bobwhites. This, of course, means that there is no real singles hunting as for bobwhites after a covey rise. The covey is always under the leadership of one old bird, either the hen or the cock.

There is one exception when a covey of huns will not flush in unison, and that's when the birds are still young. It's almost as if the young birds lack the discipline. In reality, it probably takes some time for the birds to become welded into one unit. The only times I've seen huns flush in twos or threes have been in August when working young dogs, or during the hunting season when encountering a late hatch brood, perhaps the hen's second attempt at nesting after the first clutch was pre-dated by crows, skunk, or fox.

In the late season, several family coveys frequently join into one covey. This is particularly true if the family coveys have shrunk to a handful of birds. Huns instinctively know that there is safety in numbers. A covey of huns is never without at least one sentinel.

Huns, unlike pheasants for example, always run from heavier cover into lighter cover. The reason is simple. Huns are small birds. They cannot cope with dense cover as can a pheasant. But also, huns rely on eyesight and speed of flight to get away from ground predators, and that includes hunters. In sparse cover, huns can see a hunter or a fox approach much farther than from a stand of tall grass. They can also flush easier in light cover. A dog has an easier time pinning a covey of huns in a stubble than he has in a thin pasture.

In the early fall, huns, of course, hold much better than they do later in the season. Experience counts. The birds become warier. But the cover in the fall is also less dense.

When a covey rises, the air literally seems to explode into wings and feathers. The rise is noisy from the frantic wingbeat, and the birds call with squeaking chirps. The birds fly fast and straight, although on the rise, the covey always seems to change direction shortly after takeoff.

Huns flush with considerably greater speed than pheasants or sharptails, but probably a bit slower than bobwhites. Yet they fly as fast as quail and perhaps even faster when in full flight. On the first flush, the birds seldom fly much over 300 yards, unless it's late in the season or they've been shot at quite a bit. So it's a good idea to watch the covey because it may be possible to relocate.

Gunning for Huns and Chukars

When gunning for huns in the East, I have seen birds flush from a wheat stubble but fly into a field of alfalfa or clover. Alfalfa and clover are thick cover where the birds will hold well, even late in the season.

Huns, like most gallinaceous game birds, have a daily routine. In the mornings they may nibble on green, dew-soaked grass and tender shoots, but they don't go out to feed until the dew is mostly dry. Huns don't like to get wet if they don't have to. They will feed until late morning and siesta until midafternoon. In hot weather they may seek shade for their midday rest.

They again begin feeding in midafternoon and continue until dusk. If you encounter a covey at dusk and scatter the birds into two or three bunches, they will start to call each other almost immediately upon landing. Huns use the same call in spring evenings, just before the mating season. A hunter who wants to scout for huns can do no better than to go out in spring. Where you hear a pair of huns calling in spring, there's bound to be a covey in fall.

Chukars are also covey birds. And they're great runners— even better than huns or pheasants. Yet they seldom run down-hill, and if they do it's never for long. Chukars run uphill and fly down. Every chukar hunter must take this into account when mapping his strategy.

Chukars are, in many ways, harder to find than huns. The habitat in which they live is responsible. It is vast and uniform in its cover. Any patch of sagebrush may have birds loafing under it during midday, and any patch of cheatgrass may have a covey feeding in it.

But a hunter who knows the habit of chukars will be able to select the places to look for them. You won't encounter chukars deep in the flats of valleys. Chukars are seldom far from hill-sides and slopes. Slopes with southern exposures are generally the best bet because they frequently remain free of snow, or certainly have less of it. Hunting on southern slopes may not be critical during the early season, but later it is.

THE SHOTGUN

Although chukars don't need cultivated grains for food, that doesn't mean they will pass it up if it is close to their hillside home. In some areas of the West, chukars can be hunted on the edges of grain fields where the birds feed. This is particularly true in eastern Washington.

But much of the Western chukar country is almost a semidesert of sage and cheatgrass—too dry and rough for grain growing. The birds inhabit land so rocky and steep that cattle cannot even be run on it.

In dry weather, chukars will always be found near water. Stream beds in narrow valleys are ideal places to locate birds. You can walk on the bottom and jump birds up or at least see them run up the slope. Even on vertical cliffs that a hunter would have to scale with toes and fingertips, chukars will scramble up and hop from one ledge to another with the surefootedness of a mountain goat.

In wet weather when every water hole has water and the streams are running, chukars scatter over a wider area. They don't need to hang out near creek bottoms then. They also become harder to find.

Good places to look for chukars are grassy steps or ledges near the tops of hillside slopes or canyon walls. In such spots, the birds are protected from wind. There is always some spot that catches the sun in cold weather and offers shade if it's hot. Such areas are frequently close to water at the bottom of the canyon or valley. To reach it, all the birds have to do is cup their wings and sail down.

Besides recognizing chukar habitat, a chukar hunter must also recognize the bird's tracks and call. Tracks in soft sand and dust are a sure sign that at least one covey is in the area. Good places to look for tracks are near water.

Chukars are vocal birds. At times they call to each other almost constantly. When a covey scatters, particularly at dusk, the birds are bound to call one another. To a hunter in strange chukar country, the call of a chukar is sweet music indeed.

Many chukar hunters find binoculars useful. It is, at times,

Gunning for Huns and Chukars

possible to glass up a covey of chukars as it is mule deer or desert bighorns. A hunter should stick to ridges with care and not expose himself to the skyline. Chukars have an amazing sense of vision. They can spot a moving hunter a mile away.

On approaching a ridge, a hunter should glass down the slopes and, if the valley or canyon is narrow, the slope or wall across. He should not look for bluish-gray birds, because chukars in the distance look more like tiny gray sparrows. Needless to say, when chukars are feeding or running they are easier to spot than when they are loafing in the shade.

Chukars nearly always have a daily pattern. They will move from a high slope or canyon wall lower down into a patch of cheatgrass, or even to the edge of a grain stubble to feed sometime after sunrise. They will move about feeding until late morning and then leg it up a slope partway to loaf by rock piles or sagebrush. In some areas they may loaf down at the base of the slope or canyon wall. They can even loaf right in the stubble if they haven't been hunted hard.

The second feeding period comes in the afternoon, but before dusk the birds will move uphill to roost for the night. At some point in the day they will go to water. Mornings and late afternoons are the usual watering periods, but sometimes the birds like to water right after feeding in the morning and afternoon.

A hunter must plan his hunting strategy around the chukar's schedule and hunt where the birds are apt to be during that particular time of day. The second thing a hunter must never do is think that he can run birds down as they leg it up the hill. By the time you get up the ridge, they will have flown down the other side and be running up the next slope. A hunter must outwit chukars or he won't get much shooting. In fact, he probably won't get any shooting at all. Nobody gets much shooting. Chukars are not easy to outwit, and impossible to run down by stamina alone.

Chukars can be walked down on flats or even on mild slopes where the cover is good. Whenever possible, a hunter should

THE SHOTGUN

approach the birds from downhill, knowing full well that this will force the birds to flush and fly down, thus giving a shot. The easiest time to hunt the birds is when they are feeding. They are generally in thicker cover then and hold better.

Guns and Loads

There isn't much dispute about the best shot size for both huns and chukars. Most hunters prefer 7½s, but there may be some that like 6s for chukars. The load should be a stiff one, with a full 1¼ ounces in a 12 gauge. If a 20 gauge is used, then a baby magnum of 1⅛ ounces is better than the standard 1 ounce of shot. Huns and chukars are frequently taken at long-ish ranges, so plenty of shot is needed for good, dense patterns.

The gauge of the gun is not overly important. Most hunters prefer 12s, but 20s are popular with many because 20-gauge guns are lighter. No chukar hunter wants to carry a 7-pound gun if he can get away with one that weighs a pound less. The action is less important, but probably pumps and semiautomatics predominate. Doubles, particularly over-unders, are increasing in popularity, though, because the newer models are generally lighter than pumps or autoloaders.

The modified choke is probably the best all-around choke for huns and chukars. But late in the season, when the birds hold less, some hunters prefer full chokes. This is another reason why double-barreled guns are increasing in popularity. They offer an instant selection of chokes, or an open choke for the first shot when the covey rises and a tighter choke for the second.

Most hunters prefer a combination of modified and full chokes in their double-barreled guns. But improved cylinder and modified is a good combination for huns early in the season. There are hunters who even prefer improved cylinder in one barrel for the close shots and full choke in the second.

Gunning for Huns and Chukars

Chukars can be hunted with reasonable success without a dog, but a dog can still be an important asset. For one thing, any dog that retrieves is valuable. A wing-tipped chukar is difficult for a man to chase down, even if he can see it running uphill. And there are times when shot chukars fall 200 yards down a hillside. A dog that can mark fallen birds and retrieve will save a weary hunter many steps.

Good retrieving ability is also a valuable asset when hunting huns. A wing-tipped hun also runs, but not as much as a chukar or a pheasant. A hun tends to sulk more and twist and swerve. But that makes it just as hard to find. Even a dead hun can be hard to find in a thick cover of grass, particularly if the hunter concentrates on making a double and does not mark where the first bird falls. A dog's nose can always find it.

Pointing dogs are best for both chukars and huns. This is simply because a pointing dog covers more range and therefore is bound to find more birds. For hun hunting, a wide-ranging dog such as a pointer is hard to beat. In fact, for huns the pointer is the ideal dog. Huns also usually hold much better than chukars. Early in the season in good cover such as barley or wheat stubble, a covey of huns can hold very well.

There are occasions when chukars will hold fairly tight as well. This is usually when they are feeding in dense cheatgrass or wheat stubble. Another place where chukars hold is on the edge of a ridge, as if the birds were hoping that they wouldn't have to flush and fly down. The value of a pointing dog in a chukar hunt frequently comes not from solid points on pinned coveys of birds, but because the dog indicates by flash points or creeping forward that the birds are running ahead. The hunter can then work out a strategy that will earn him some shooting.

Coveys of huns or chukars give off a lot of scent. I've seen keen-nosed dogs point both species at distances of 60 or 70 yards. But even this is not enough when the birds are wild or the cover is very sparse!

THE SHOTGUN

10

Dove Hunting
Know-How

The dove is a bird that rates high on many hunters' lists. It is a popular game bird in many states, as well as in Mexico. Be it the common mourning dove or the bigger whitewing, this bird prefers a moderate climate. It lives in the North during summer and migrates southward when winter is near at hand.

The dove is a small and rapid-flying bird with long, pointed wings and short legs. In full flight it has been clocked at 60 miles per hour. To be present at the right time and the right place is the secret to dove hunting.

Much sought after by the wing-shooting sportsmen is the mourning dove, *Zenaidura macroura*. It is the most common of the doves and very widespread. The mourning dove is found mainly in open woodlands, farmlands, grain fields, stubble, and along roadsides. Our only dove with a white-edged pointed tail and marked with a body of buff gray with a bluish cast to the wings, the mourning dove prefers to live in the temperate zones.

Another popular member of the dove family, a bit larger than the mourning dove, is the white-winged dove *(Zenaida asiatica)*. In the United States, the whitewing is found much in the desert country of Arizona and Texas, and usually at places where water is available. Early in the morning (at least in the West) and again in the evening, the hunter who discovers where the whitewing is feeding should be able to find some good pass shooting. This requires a shotgun with a modified choke and No. 7½ shot. (In much of the East, dove hunting before noon is illegal.)

Where to Hunt

A dove will feed on the ground, mainly on grain, seeds, and fruits. Its long wings and powerful flight muscles make it a strong and swift-flying bird. It can be a tricky target as it flies about seeking both food and water—dipping, dodging, and swerving in erratic flight patterns.

In many places, especially in the South and Southcentral states, the birds are found in goodly numbers. Opening day brings out many sportsmen for the first shoot.

Flights of mourning doves and whitewings are plentiful in farmlands along rivers and streams, while cultivated fields farther south will also hold an abundance of them. They may be found anywhere from the Gulf of Mexico to Canada in the heat of summer, and seem to be constantly in the air. But there comes a time when the migrating doves from the North join with the Southern flocks and head for the feeding grounds en masse, offering shooting that is very rewarding.

Many hunters return year after year to their own special spots. These, of course, will be places that have proven to be consistently good for doves in previous years. This means places where the hunting pressure has been light, the food is abundant, water is available, and the location is remote from populated centers.

It pays to stick to such proven grounds, even if they may be somewhat hard to get to. First-hand information about hotspots can also be discovered by getting in touch with local sporting-goods dealers or with local hunters who are enthusiastic about doves. A phone call to any game warden in these places is also a good idea.

The common pigeon, also known as the rock dove, can be found especially around farms where it often roosts in the eaves of barns. Photo: Leonard Lee Rue IV.

The mourning dove is considered a songbird in much of the northern tier of the United States, but is a challenging gamebird elsewhere. Photo: Leonard Lee Rue III.

The white-winged dove can supply some of the trickiest game of all with its speed and darting, weaving flight habits. More shells are probably expended on doves than on any other bird; one experienced hunter figured that the doves he served on the table one night costed out to $14 per ounce, but the sport in shooting them more than outweighed the cost. Photo: Leonard Lee Rue III.

Dove Hunting Know-How

Mostly, the more prolific areas will require some traveling to reach. But if the birds are there in sufficient numbers, this is well worthwhile. One way to find where they are is to drive through the country scanning the countryside with a pair of binoculars.

How to Hunt Doves

Where there are reservoirs, ponds, streams, and stock tanks, doves should be on hand. But check the condition of these watering places before planning to hunt there. During harvest time, when the watering holes and irrigation ditches tend to be well filled, you can expect fine prospects for dove shooting. Early in the season, plenty of shooting may develop with large numbers of birds tracing back and forth between feeding fields and watering places.

Because doves follow a rather definite route in their comings and goings, they offer pass shooting that keeps the hunter on his toes. As they wing overhead in their dodging flights, the shotgunner should find a strategic spot along the flight lanes and take them as they come.

One mistake many hunters make in this type of pass shooting is firing at out-of-range birds. Some shooters also commit the error of not using enough lead on doves, especially the high fliers. If the shot is possible, the gunner must swing far enough in front to put the bird in the middle of the shot pattern, or the shell will be wasted. On opening day, many of the shots will be easy. But this condition soon changes as the birds take to the high lanes and become difficult targets.

An ideal place for the hunter to station himself for effective pass shooting is between the dove's nesting-resting place and water. With grooves for nesting and water in adjacent irrigation ditches, along with a food source not far away, the birds will be trading back and forth. If the hunter is able to find a spot that is partially concealed by brush and foliage, he should account for a busy day of shooting at the fast fliers. One of the problems is retrieving fallen birds, and for this purpose the Brittany spaniel proves quite suitable. This is a dog that has the game at heart and will do his utmost to find downed doves.

The birds are attractive early in the morning and will head for water and any available cultivated field, darting up and down from the ground in their feeding. They may rest in between times on wires and the topmost branches of trees. Along the dirt roads, at times, they stop and pick up grit to grind their food.

The time to be after the birds, where it is legal, is just after breakfast. From early to midmorning the doves will be looking for grain, coming and going in busy fashion. Sometime before noon they will head back for the brush and trees. About midafternoon they're out again, feeding until dusk.

In country that is on the dry side, the doves will be close to any creek bed or irrigation ditch where the hunter can station himself in the brush and target the birds as they fly ahead and round about. Many hunters like to hunt along the fencerows or the edges of grain fields in more open areas.

Where a party of men is after doves, they can work their way through the stubble and weeds as the doves are feeding and target the birds that fly up ahead. Hunting into the wind is the best procedure, and will produce more sporty shooting.

Guns and Loads

Because the dove is a small bird, it doesn't take too much shot to down it. Most experienced dove hunters use No. 7½ or 8 shot on fairly close targets. The 12 gauge is favored by many dove hunters where the shots run to distance, but the 20 is quite adequate. In either the 12 or 20 gauge, the choke most used is the modified, with the improved cylinder being the next choice.

Dove Hunting Know-How

11

Wild Turkey Comeback

There seems to be a difference of opinion as to whether or not the wild turkey belongs in a book on upland birds, for turkey hunting takes on all the aspects of big-game hunting. As with deer and elk, for instance, the best results on this game bird are had when you stalk it carefully; or wait in a blind, hoping the turkey will wander in range of your shotgun.

The wild turkey has enjoyed a remarkable comeback. At the turn of the century, it had dwindled and even disappeared over much of its historic range. But under modern wildlife management it has been restored to such numbers that more than thirty states have this magnificent bird on their open-season list.

Where you hunt it, the wild turkey is found in sequestered spots. The best time to hunt is in the early morning following a heavy rain. The birds seem to prefer this weather, and the soft ground is an aid to the hunter in his quiet stalk through the woods. Prehunt planning is all important. Turkey hunting has changed radically since the old days. In years gone by the birds were seen much in their domain, being plentiful and none too cautious. No more. This bird is now wary and educated, and desirous of no other company than that of his own species.

You must do plenty of research to find recent turkey range, and when you've located the birds, must hunt them like the whitetail deer. Get up early in the morning for the best hunting, and then keep at it all day if nothing shows. You may bag a gobbler the first day out; then again you may draw a blank for some time.

Description

The wild turkey, *Meleagris gallopavo*, is a handsome bird and a prize for any upland gunner. It looks pretty much like the domestic bronze turkey and is of the same species, but is leaner and has a richer bronze coloration. Black, touched with a red-green iridescence, is the basic color.

The wings and tail are a copper-bronze, and the wing feathers are a barred black and white. All males (and a few females) have a coarse black beard suspended from the crop region. In size the male runs to 48 inches, the female to 36, and they both have a wingspread of some 5 feet.

The male has a sparsely feathered head and upper neck with heavy deposits called caruncles. The wild tom is not usually the large bird you find among some domestic turkeys, weighing about 15 pounds on the average, but it can go as high as 20 pounds.

Habitat

The wild turkey is a forest bird that shuns the clearings in feeding, a key to where it can best be sought. Its diet consists of acorns, nuts, seeds, grasses, roots, leaf buds, fruits, berries, insects, and some small crustaceans.

Wild Turkey Comeback

Since time immemorial the wild turkey has symbolized sport of a singular nature. It is our largest game bird, and formerly was found in most of the eastern, central, southern, and southwestern parts of North America.

Today the wild turkey holds to the more sequestered spots of his domain with the backlands of the mountainous areas— such as the Appalachians—taking first place. In such country they will be found on ridges and in high cover that contains a good crop of beechnut or acorn mast on the leafy ground.

You will find them here in the coves and glens, and they can be hunted by scouting out their feeding places and then waiting for them in brushy concealment, or by using a call, or both.

The hunter must stalk the turkey quietly and slowly, and wait for the game to appear in some logical feeding location, reaching the area before dawn, if possible. In the South, wild turkeys will head for grassy little glades between clumps of palmettos and palms, where the hunter can hide out and wait.

Where to Hunt

The wild turkey can be hunted in many states. Some have a spring hunting season, but the majority have an open turkey season from the middle of October into late winter. Some recommended turkey-hunting states are Maryland, Pennsylvania, Oklahoma, West Virginia, Mississippi, Texas, Wyoming, and California. Conservation department men in the various wild turkey hunting states will be able to pinpoint turkey strongholds.

By instinct the turkey is easily frightened, quick to detect anything foreign to its surroundings, and has unbelievably sharp eyesight. The bird must feed, though. That's the secret to hunting turkey. Like so much other game, the turkey is a creature of set routine. Led by a large male gobbler, the flock usually will start from the roost early in the morning. Dropping from their secluded perches, usually in evergreen trees, they

Here is a sight turkey hunters would love to see but mostly don't— wild turkey toms strutting in an Oklahoma woodlot. Photo: F. B. McMurry, U.S. Fish and Wildlife Service.

will begin walking toward their feeding grounds, and once finding it will stay around the spot most of the day, heading back for the roost toward dusk.

The all-around woodsman is often the hunter who will score with the wild turkey. He will take time to discover the turkey hangout; and then stalk the game with meticulous care, or hunt from a camouflaged blind. The old hand at calling will also stand a fine chance of getting his bird. But whatever the method, it is highly advisable to be Johnny-on-the-spot at the crack of dawn. Be there when the birds are dropping silently

Wild Turkey Comeback

from their roosts, and try to find them before they become too active.

Expert Guide and a Good Turkey Call

On the whole, turkey hunting takes on the aspect of a squirrel or deer still-hunt. Many hunters use a call, usually of local origin, with fine results. Two good manufactured calls are put out by Burnham Brothers, Marble Falls, Texas, and by Bill Tannehill, Staunton, Virginia. But whether the caller is a

A wild turkey tom, as indicated by the so-called beard hanging down from the midchest area. Some females also grow such beards, and are usually considered legal game even in seasons when females are otherwise protected. Photo: Leonard Lee Rue III.

A Rio Grande turkey—native to the Southwest and Mexico but introduced elsewhere in the United States—walks alongside an Arkansas lake. Photo: W. F. Kubichek, U.S. Fish and Wildlife Service.

manufactured article or a homemade affair, it must be used with discretion.

Naturally, if an expert guide is doing the calling he will know how to lure the gobblers within range. The usual method is to hide in a good feeding area, remain very quiet, send out a few plaintive notes (like the hen calling the male) and hope for the best.

The right call, if turkeys are within hearing distance, will often lure the flock or a lone gobbler close to the blind. An old hand at turkey calling is your best assurance here. But the amateur caller, with the help of a good teacher, or by following

A magnificent tom turkey in full display before his harem. The fatty growths hanging down below his bill are the caruncles. Photo: Denise Hendershot, % Leonard Rue Enterprises.

Wild Turkey Comeback

the instructions accompanying the turkey call, can put on a convincing performance. One of the best calls, and fairly easy to use, is the box call. Properly made of the right wood and dimensions, this call is superior to any other.

Not all turkeys are wild and crafty. Many are taken by chance. Instances have been cited where the bird actually was an easy mark, sometimes holding to cover that did not begin to shield it, or roosting openly in a tree with the hunter clearly visible. But not often. With the wild turkey it is usually a question of pitting your skill against a sagacious quarry, with the reservation, however, that in the main it is no harder to bag a wild turkey than any other bird, providing a man is careful, has the proper load, and can get a fairly open shot.

Gun, Load, and How to Shoot

When the hunter does get a shot, he must try for the head or neck. The wild turkey will carry a lot of lead if the shot is not placed just right. The feathers are hard, and to top it off the turkey is skillful enough to escape even when crippled.

It's best to get an aim on the gobbler as quickly as he shows his head, then fire. Make a beeline for the spot if the turkey drops, and grab him quickly in case he is just stunned.

Most successful turkey hunters carry a full-choked 12-gauge shotgun loaded with high-velocity, long-range loads of No. 4 or 6 shot. The 6s are used to take a head shot on a standing turkey, while the 4s are used on body shots at a running or flying bird. In states where it is legal, some hunters use rifles. A .22 rimfire is not a good turkey rifle except in the case of head shots. More favored rifles include the .22 rimfire Magnum or such varmint cartridges as the .22 Hornet and the .222, hand-loaded with bullets of tough construction and lower velocities, so that not much meat will be destroyed.

12

Rabbit and Squirrel— America's Most Popular Game

No book on hunting the uplands with shotgun and rifle would be complete without a chapter on the great American tradition of rabbit and squirrel hunting. The most favored game of upland hunters is not the pheasant, the quail, the grouse, or even the dove—but the cottontail rabbit and the squirrel. Probably more shotgun shells and .22 rifle cartridges are expended on these two game species than on all upland game birds put together.

In bumper years, Missouri hunters alone have bagged up to 6,000,000 cottontails per year. Other top rabbit states include Indiana, with an annual state bag of 2,500,000 cottontails. A bag of the same magnitude is taken in Kentucky, while Ohio hunters take up to 3,500,000 rabbits per year.

The squirrel is the number two game species, just behind the cottontail. The reason is that the squirrel is not as widely distributed as the cottontail. But in those states with high squirrel populations, bushytails frequently outrank cottontails as the most sought-after game. In such states as Arkansas, Kentucky, Tennessee, Virginia, West Virginia, Mississippi, South Carolina, and Louisiana, squirrel hunting is more popular than rabbit hunting.

Distribution and Habitat

Gray and fox squirrels are the major game squirrels in North America, but they are not our only squirrels. The small red squirrel of the evergreen forests of New England, the Great Lakes States, the Mountain States, and Canada is seldom hunted. Neither is the tassel-eared Albert squirrel of Arizona, which is just too local to be an important game species. Westerners also lack a strong squirrel-hunting tradition. Because of this, the handsome Western gray squirrel of California, Oregon, and Washington is also not much hunted.

The Eastern gray squirrel (*Sciurus carolinensis*) is smaller than the fox squirrel (*Sciurus niger*). It weighs about 1¼ pounds on the average, while an adult fox squirrel runs twice that. As the name suggests, the gray squirrel is predominantly gray in color with a light underbelly. In the northern part of its range, a black color phase occurs with fair frequency. The black squirrels are not a separate species; indeed, squirrels of gray or black color can appear in the same litter.

The fox squirrel is also highly variable in color. Over most of its range it has a rusty-yellowish—foxy—color, explaining the name fox squirrel. But along the Atlantic coast in Delaware and Maryland it may be steel gray. In the Southeast it may run almost black. Its pelt is more hairy and unkempt in appearance than that of the smaller gray squirrel.

The fox squirrel is found from Minnesota and Michigan south to Florida and Texas. Its Western distribution includes the Dakotas and Iowa, while its Eastern range runs to Pennsylvania and even Maryland.

The Eastern gray squirrel is popular among hunters if only because it is widespread and populous enough to provide good hunting, yet elusive enough to provide challenging sport. Photo: Leonard Lee Rue III.

The gray squirrel ranges from New England and southern Canada south to Florida and westward to Texas and North Dakota. Not found in the Mountain states, the gray squirrel is an animal of mature hardwood forests. In the hill country of the South the oak-hickory forests are viewed as ideal gray squirrel woods, as long as they have not been burned, cut over, or pastured. Good squirrel woods contain a mixture of trees in type and size, but there must be an abundance of mature trees that bear mast and nut crops and have plenty of cavities for dens.

Fox squirrels prefer smaller, more open woodlots. They are not so arboreal as gray squirrels. In fact, when in trees they appear to be clumsier than the gray squirrel. Fox squirrels can even thrive in farming country with no woodlots, as long as there are trees in the fencerows.

Rabbit and Squirrel–America's Most Popular Game

Cottontails can live almost anywhere that has enough cover in the form of weeds and brush. The cottontail is an extremely adaptable animal. Even in areas where there is not much cover, rabbits can still survive if there are plenty of woodchuck holes.

There are essentially four species of cottontails. The Eastern cottontail *(Sylvilagus floridanus)* is found in brush, forest edge, slashcovered woodlots, weedy fields, and ravines from the Rocky Mountains eastward to the Atlantic Ocean and from southern Saskatchewan and Alberta down into Florida and Mexico.

The mountain cottontail *(Sylvilagus nuttalli)* prefers brushy and grassy east and west slopes of the Rocky Mountains from Alberta to New Mexico and Arizona, including the Pacific States. The desert cottontail *(Sylvilagus auduboni)* lives in arid grasslands and scrub desert from western Texas to the

By far the most popular game animal in the Western hemisphere is the cottontail rabbit. And despite the 25 million or so rabbits taken by hunters each year, hunters are far from being the rabbit's greatest enemy. It seems probable that housecats account for the most rabbit fatalities, with other predators ranking well ahead of man, who is also outranked by such vagaries as disease and the weather. Photo: Leonard Lee Rue III.

THE SHOTGUN

Pacific, and as far north as Montana and North Dakota. The fourth species, the New England cottontail (Sylvilagus transitionalis), prefers forested and brushy areas in the hill country of New England, right down the Appalachians to Alabama.

We have four other species of rabbits in America as well. These are not called cottontails, but like cottontails they belong to the genus Sylvilagus. The pygmy rabbit (Sylvilagus idahoensis) is the smallest of the rabbits, seldom weighing more than a pound. It is found in the sagebrush country from central California to southeastern Washington, eastward into Utah and Montana. The pygmy rabbit lacks the white "cotton" tail.

Another rabbit that lacks the white tail is the brush rabbit (Sylvilagus bachmani) that lives in the chaparral from Baja California north into Oregon. The brush rabbit is also quite small, with an average weight of 1½ pounds. The marsh rabbit (Sylvilagus palustris) is a bunny of wet bottomlands and swamps from South Carolina to Florida and Alabama. It resembles the cottontail a great deal; it even has a conspicuous white tail. Most hunters would not be able to tell the marsh rabbit from the eastern cottontail.

The swamp rabbit or canecutter (Sylvilagus aquaticus) is larger than the cottontail. Canecutters have been known to weigh up to 6 pounds and their average weight is over 4 pounds. This makes them the largest rabbit we have. The swamp rabbit is found in swamps and river bottoms along the Mississippi drainage system from southern Illinois and Indiana south to Louisiana and Mississippi. From there it ranges eastward into Georgia and westward into Texas and Oklahoma.

The snowshoe rabbit (Lepus americanus), a popular game animal among the houndsmen of New England and the northern Great Lakes States, is not technically a rabbit, but a hare. One major difference between the rabbits and the hares is that the young of rabbits are born blind and naked, while the young of hares are born furred and with their eyes open. Hares can hop about shortly after birth.

Rabbit and Squirrel—America's Most Popular Game

Hares never use holes and burrows as do rabbits. They never hole up, even when pursued by predators or hounds. For this reason, they are a favorite with houndsmen.

The snowshoe hare is closely related to the Western jackrabbits, which are also hares and not rabbits. But unlike the jackrabbits, the snowshoe hare is a game animal with a closed season during spring and summer throughout its range. The jackrabbits are not game animals, but rather agricultural pests and are seldom protected. Since they are thus considered varmints rather than game, they will not be mentioned further in this book.

The snowshoe hare is an animal of young evergreen forests. Its range extends from Alaska south into the Mountain States, including northern California and even as far south as New Mexico; and from northern Canada down to North Dakota, the northern Great Lakes States, New England, and along the Appalachian Mountains as far south as Tennessee.

The snowshoe hare is uniquely adapted to snow. It gets its name from its large feet, which are designed to carry the animal over deep snows. In the fall it also turns white. For this reason it is sometimes called the varying hare, because its color varies from brown in summer to white in winter.

The snowshoe rabbit, so called, is not really a rabbit but a hare, a related species that differs from rabbits in part in that their young are born in an advanced state of development (new-born rabbits are blind, furless, and helpless). The true name of the snowshoe is varying hare, from the animal's characteristic of changing its brownish or grayish coloration of the summer months to a snow-white camouflage in winter. Photo: Leonard Lee Rue III.

The best time to hunt squirrels is in the early morning, particularly in summer or during early fall when the days are warm. Squirrels, grays in particular, are early risers on mild days. By midmorning squirrels have generally stopped feeding and den up.

In late fall, when the temperature has plummeted, squirrels are not as prone to getting up with the sun. Then, in fact, they normally wait a bit, until the sun has warmed things up. Hard rain also keeps squirrels in their dens, as does high wind. Squirrels, however, don't seem to mind gentle breezes or soft gentle rains. A good time to hunt squirrels is right after a heavy rain when the sun begins to shine. The squirrels will be out feeding in full force, and the wet leaves make for quiet walking. Squirrel dogs also work better right after a rain, because scenting conditions are good.

Squirrels, particularly grays, also become more active in the midafternoon on hot days. Temperatures are cooler then. But fox squirrels won't stay out for long. They are generally back in their dens by late afternoon.

Another good time to hunt squirrels is just before a weather change, such as a winter snowstorm that may last a day. The bushytails are active then, trying to get full stomachs with which to last out the bad weather. The day after the storm, even if it has dumped a foot of snow, is a good time as well. The squirrels will be out feeding after a day of fasting.

Still hunting, so popular with many whitetail deer hunters, is also popular among squirrel hunters. In fact, the walk-and-wait system is probably more effective on bushytails than on whitetails.

In this hunting technique, the hunter walks slowly and quietly through squirrel woods, looking and listening. He looks for a flick of a tail or a piece of a head or ear showing from behind a tree trunk, or perhaps even for a branch swaying on a windless day. He listens for the swish of leaves, falling debris from acorns being gnawed, and the sharp bark of a squirrel. The hunter stops frequently because he can see and hear better when he is still.

This walk-and-wait system is best when the leaves are damp and the hunter won't make much noise. When the leaves are crisp and noisy, the hunter is better taking a stand in promising squirrel woods. Oak and hickory groves with a good acorn or nut crop are ideal. So is a hardwood ridge near a cornfield.

Floating down a lazy creek or river in a canoe or flat-bottomed johnboat is a squirrel-hunting technique that is popular with an increasing number of upland hunters. It frequently gets the hunter away from woodlots near roads into seldom-hunted river bottoms. It can also be combined with fishing. The floating squirrel hunter with a shotgun can also bag the odd duck.

At times, squirrels respond well to a call. There are two types of squirrel calls on the market. One is mouth-operated; the other is mechanical. The purpose of the call is not to call the squirrel within shooting range, but to locate it by making it answer by barking or chattering. Fox squirrels respond better to calls than grays, but young grays will frequently bark back.

Squirrels can be hunted successfully with a dog. There are no special breeds of dogs for squirrel hunting. In fact, most squirrel dogs are mongrels and feists of various sorts. Generally the best squirrel dogs seem to have some terrier blood.

All a squirrel dog needs is a sense of smell good enough to pick up a fresh trail and follow it to a tree. Once the squirrel is treed, all the dog must do is bark a few times to reveal its location and look upward in case the squirrel makes a leap from one tree to another. If the squirrel starts doing that, the dog must follow. Most squirrel dogs are not trained in the formal sense. They simply pick things up on their own.

Rabbit hunting reaches its zenith with a hound or two, generally a beagle. The technique is simple and the same, regardless of the rabbit hunted—cottontail, swamp rabbit, or snowshoe hare.

THE SHOTGUN

A hunter and his hounds walk through likely looking rabbit cover. The hound probes every nook and cranny to get a chase started. A rabbit hound, to be successful, must have three qualities—a good nose, know-how in finding rabbits, and persistence on the trail. If it has a good voice as well, the hunt becomes that much more enjoyable.

A rabbit with a hound on its track is nowhere near so crafty as a fox or a coon, but it does have some tricks—it will run back and forth on its tracks and then leap sideways to confuse the hounds and it will twist and circle in a thicket so that trails crisscross each other without rhyme or reason.

There isn't a hound born that hasn't lost a rabbit track at least a few times in its career. Young hounds lose trails with regularity. The only way they can learn is through experience. Nonetheless rabbits are uncomplicated animals. They spend most of their lives in one area. Biologists call this the "home range." The home range of a cottontail is probably less than three or four acres. The home ranges of the canecutter and the snowshoe hare are much bigger.

The home range is significant to a rabbit hunter. It is the reason why rabbits circle back to where they were jumped by the hound—a rabbit is reluctant to leave its home range. Once it does, it is a stranger in unfamiliar terrain.

Since the cottontail has a smaller home range, the hounds "bring it home" earlier and quicker. A cottontail seldom runs more than 100 yards before turning. Snowshoes and canecutters run in much bigger circles because their home ranges are larger. Occasionally a snowshoe can take hounds out of hearing range.

When a rabbit is jumped by hounds the hunter should take a stand somewhere near the point where the hounds started the chase. The stand should cover the logical places a rabbit may cross; for example, open narrows between two thickets. The stand should, if possible, give a good, clean shot.

Cottontails, being animals of brushy thick cover, don't really like to run across the open. Snowshoes, however, don't seem to

Rabbit and Squirrel–America's Most Popular Game

mind. They rely on speed and a camouflage of white on a background of snow for protection. Canecutters don't mind taking to the water. They are good swimmers.

The game bag is always heavier if there are two or three hunters. It is difficult for one hunter to pick the right place to wait for the rabbit to circle. But when there are two or three hunters involved, one is almost certain to get a shot when the rabbit comes by.

The all-time favorite rabbit hound is the beagle. In fact, cottontails and beagles go together like bacon and eggs. The basset can also be a good rabbit hound, but it is difficult to find a basset from hunting stock these days. Most are bred for pets and dog shows.

For cottontail hunting, the hound should be slow and persistent. A fast hound will push the rabbit too fast and drive it into a hole. Even with canecutters, which seldom ever hole up, and snowshoe hares, which never go underground except when wounded, a fast hound will drive a rabbit farther before it circles. But many hunters prefer bigger, longer legged hounds than beagles for snowshoes because small hounds have a tough time in deep snow. Hunting the snowshoe hare is nearly always a winter sport.

Rabbits can also be hunted without hounds. A hunter can jump his own rabbits from thickets and brushpiles. The technique here is to walk slowly through promising rabbit cover and investigate every possible place where a cottontail can hide. The trick is to stop frequently. Cottontails rely on camouflage as their first line of defense. They will stay in their beds as long as they think you will walk by. Once you stop and they feel that they've been seen, they will bolt.

For this kind of rabbit hunting, a flushing dog is useful. I know hunters who use their Labs and springers regularly, and with surprising success.

Another technique for hunting cottontails is to take a stand near a good cover or thicket at dusk. This is particularly effective in winter. The rabbits frequently come out of their beds and holes before dark. This is a fine way for a rifleman to hunt them.

Still another fine way for a rifleman to hunt cottontails is to stalk them right after a snowfall. The snow makes the rabbit stand out more, even in thick, bramble-choked covers. This type of hunting calls for lots of looking and little walking. Don't look for an entire rabbit, but rather part of one. The dark eyes are frequently a giveaway.

Cottontails will generally sit in more open cover on mild, sunny days. They prefer hillsides and sides of ravines with southern exposures that catch most of the sun and are sheltered from the wind.

Canecutters can also be walked up, but because they live in even thicker cover than cottontails, this is not a very effective method of hunting them. Snowshoe hares can also be walked up, but it is much easier in the fall before the snow comes. They hold much better. Once the snow is on the ground and the hares are white, they become as wild as a buck whitetail.

Guns and Loads

Squirrel hunters are divided about the best gun for their sport. The shotgun is probably favored by most because running shots can be taken. But many still hunters and hunters who prefer to take a stand use rifles. Accurate scope-sighted .22s are most commonly used.

The riflemen are evenly divided between those who prefer .22 hollow points and those who swear by solids. No one argues that for body-shot squirrels hollow points are more effective in producing quick kills, but many proponents of solids feel that hollow points waste too much meat.

Probably the best bet is to use hollow points and concentrate on head shots to avoid wasting edible meat. But if a body shot is taken, it's wiser to waste a bit of meat than to have a mortally wounded squirrel run off into a den. The whole animal is then wasted.

Rabbit and Squirrel—America's Most Popular Game

A shotgun for squirrel shooting should be capable of digesting at least an ounce of shot. This lets out the 28 gauge and the .410. The choke should be fairly tight—no less than modified—and even a full is not too tight where the squirrels are fairly wild and long shots have to be taken.

There is some debate about the best shot size for squirrels. Certainly squirrels are tough little critters. No. 6 shot is probably about the best for grays, but for the larger fox squirrels even No. 4s may not be too large.

The shotgun is also the most popular firearm for rabbits. But whereas the choke for squirrels should be fairly tight, for rabbits it should be open—no more than modified, and in most instances improved cylinder is even a better bet.

Rabbits, particularly cottontails and marsh rabbits, are hunted in thick cover where a 40-yard shot is a long one indeed. Most shots are taken at a shorter range. That's why a fairly open choke is desirable. Rabbits will also be running with a tricky zigzag pattern. An open choke will make them easier to hit.

Even for snowshoes the choke should be fairly open. Although in an open woodlot it is possible to get a longer shot on occasion, most shooting will be done under 35 or 40 yards.

The gauge is not all that important, but again it's best to stick with the larger gauges—20, 16, and 12. The smaller gauges just don't pack enough shot for good, dense patterns. But at short ranges they can be used by a good shot.

The best shot size is probably No. 6, but there are some hunters who prefer 7½s for cottontails. Certainly 7½s are effective at short ranges early in the fall, before the cottontails get their winter pelage. Although 6s are the most popular choice for the larger snowshoes, there are some old-timers in the North Woods who prefer larger shot sizes—5s when they can get them or even 4s.

A rifle can be an effective rabbit gun if cottontails are stalked on winter days right after a snowfall or if you can take a stand in some rabbit-holding cover at dusk. Most of the shots taken are at sitting rabbits. There are a few riflemen around who can hit rabbits on the run with surprising accuracy.

There is, of course, only one good rifle caliber for rabbit hunting and that is .22 rimfire. Solids are quite adequate; rabbits are not hard to kill. There may be some hunters who prefer the .22 rimfire Magnum, but in my experience the .22 rimfire Magnum just destroys too much meat. It is a better choice for Western jackrabbits, which are agricultural pests and seldom eaten.

There may be the odd hunter who prefers to use his deer rifle loaded with small-game handloads for rabbits in order to gain more familiarity with his deer rifle. This isn't a bad idea. Even if you prefer to use a .22 rimfire you should choose the action type that is on your deer rifle. It makes everything less confusing.

Otherwise, the action type of the rifle is largely unimportant. Any of the repeaters are a good choice. Semiautomatics and lever actions are probably the most popular. The choice of sights is more important. The hunter should use the type of sights he is most comfortable with. But for sitting rabbits, just as for sitting squirrels, the scope sight is best, with 4x being about ideal power, because it still allows a hunter to take an off-hand shot if he has to. More power than a 4x magnifies the hand shake too much for comfortable off-hand shooting.

Even for running rabbits a scope sight can be a good choice, just as it is for deer hunting. But it must have a wide field of view so that it is easy to get onto the target and give long eye relief, so that it's easy to instantly center the eye in the scope. This means a low-power scope with 2½x being about the best choice.

These criteria let out all of the inexpensive .22 scopes. Their eye relief is just too critical and their field of view too narrow for fast shooting on rapidly moving game. Besides, there are very few 2½-power scopes made with ¾-inch tubes.

Many of today's .22 rifles are finely made guns. Most cost almost as much as center-fire rifles. It's a good idea to mount high-quality scopes on them.

Rabbit and Squirrel–America's Most Popular Game

13

Gun Dogs for Upland Game

The enjoyment of hunting upland birds can be greatly enhanced by the aid and companionship of a good bird dog. If the dog is the right type for the game and has the proper training, it will find birds that the dogless hunter would otherwise pass by. Another advantage is that an able dog will find and retrieve downed birds, saving a lot of often frustrating thrashing about in the underbrush.

Some hunters even feel that a day afield is simply not complete without one or two dogs assisting. To them, dogs and bird shooting go hand in hand.

All these accomplishments do not come easily for a young dog. But if the dog has any inclination and instinct for hunting, and if it is given the proper training, it will learn to do all this, and gladly. Most hunting dogs, like their nonhunting kin, are anxious to please their owners. After the dog has done a nice job of pointing, flushing, or retrieving, for instance, it will respond with enthusiasm to a pat on the head and a few words of appreciation.

The right dog does not, however, just happen. It takes a bit of doing at times, and sometimes a lot of luck to get just the right one. It's well to make sure the dog you are choosing is one that comes from strong hunting stock with the right breeding for the job. Show dogs may be beautiful, but for field use, a dog from hunting stock is essential.

The pureblooded puppy is a logical choice. From then on, whether you do it yourself or rely on a professional trainer, training should be started at a very early age. The puppy should be given short runs in the field from three months of age onward. This is how hunting instincts are aroused in the field.

No doubt problems will arise. Even a bird dog that has been given initial training by the breeder may prove troublesome at first. But chances are that the problems you run into will offer much incentive for you to get out of doors and help the dog with such basic lessons as listening to your voice and learning obedience commands such as "down" or "heel."

There is no need to make the lessons lengthy. A short session every day will prove sufficient for the properly bred and intelligent puppy to discover what you expect of him. Try to train the dog to respect and obey your commands. Always use a firm but friendly voice which will not frighten or alarm the dog.

It is well, also, to encourage the dog as much as possible by word and action after the successful bagging of a bird. With a little give and take, the hunting dog will catch on and obey its owner. As a general rule, it is best that only one man—the owner—handle a particular hunting dog, especially a young one.

Upland bird dogs are separated into two types: those that point and those that flush game. Many dogs of individual breeds, however, can also be taught to do jobs outside their specialties.

Gun Dogs for Upland Game

For upland hunting, both setters and pointers make excellent bird dogs. Both types are intelligent, tractable, keen scented, and have plenty of strength and stamina in the field. They are handsome dogs, and when the hot scent of sitting birds fills the air, they will freeze into immobility and present a classic point.

Both types are avid hunters—fast working, strong, and willing. Among the setters, the English setter is really outstanding. It is a proven upland bird breed and one of the oldest bird dogs used in America. English setters have wavy hair on the body and a light covering of hair on the legs. Their coloration is white, flecked with black, tan, or chestnut. A full-grown field setter stands about 2 feet tall at the withers and weighs some 45 to 55 pounds. For quail, grouse, and woodcock especially, the English setter is exceptional.

The English setter also has a capacity for affection that will lead it to any lengths in trying to please its master. Many an upland gunner will want this type not only for its ability in the field, but also for its slim, graceful lines, deep chest, and beautiful head. This is a dog that makes an able and handsome worker in field and thicket, as well as an affectionate companion at home.

Another noteworthy dog is the Irish setter, outstanding in appearance because of the mahogany-red coloration of its long hair. The Irish is a beautiful dog in the field or out of it. The Irish setter does have a tendency to willfulness at times, but has proven its worth on all types of upland birds. For quail especially, a well-trained Irish setter is a bird dog par excellence.

Also among setters is the Gordon, named after the Duke of Gordon. This breed is not seen much in the American field, but where used on birds, the Gordon setter performs well and fast. A bit smaller than the English setter, the Gordon, with its stylish appearance and performance, stands out in field trials. Its coloration is black with tan markings.

Its deep red coat makes the Irish setter, shown here retrieving a ringneck, one of the most spectacularly beautiful of all field dogs. Photo: Leonard Lee Rue III.

An English setter holds a classic point. The predominantly white color of the dog's coat makes it easy to spot even in heavy, brushy cover. Photo: Leonard Lee Rue III.

Gun Dogs for Upland Game

Unfortunately, most Irish and Gordon setters come from show lines, not field stock. So if you choose either of these breeds, make certain that your dog comes from proven hunting stock.

Equally popular to the setter is the pointer. The pointer is a great game finder. It is not as affectionate as the English setter, but its short coat makes it easier to care for in some kinds of cover.

The English pointer is a big-going dog, particularly favored for bobwhite hunting on the big plantations of the South. But the pointer can handle a variety of game—prairie grouse, Western quail, huns, chukars, and even the foxy ring-necked pheasant. The pointer is a fast-maturing dog that begins to point early. In bird-dog field trials, pointers win more silver and ribbons than any other breed. In training, the pointer needs a firm hand. It tends to be fiery and hard-headed.

Among the European gun dogs, the German wirehaired pointer is a standout. With the advantage that its wiry hair does not pick up burrs in the field, it is a robust, hard working, and fairly stocky dog. The adults weigh about 60 pounds. This dog will point and retrieve upland game and waterfowl with the best of them. Although the German wirehair has been on the American scene since the 1920s, the breed didn't really catch on until the late 1950s. It is taking the fancy of many bird hunters now, especially those who habitually hunt ringnecks, ruffed grouse, and woodcock in brushy country.

The German wirehaired pointer is a nice-looking animal in the field. Its wiry bluish-gray coat is mottled with patches ranging from solid liver to combinations of liver and brown, making it a handsome study when coming to a classic point on game. A well-trained and able German wirehair will hold birds until its owner comes up, freezing and pointing in style, and is a joy to behold when the birds are there. German wirehairs are also adept at finding and retrieving downed birds, even in heavy cover.

Another wirehaired pointing dog is the wirehaired pointing

griffon. This is the slowest and closest-ranging of all the pointing dogs. The wirehaired pointing griffon is sometimes called the Korthals griffon, after the man who developed the breed in Holland.

The griffon may not be as spectacular a dog to watch in the field as the English setter or even a good German shorthair, but it is methodical and steady. When a griffon works a cover over, it does so with absolute thoroughness. Don't expect the classic point from the griffon. But this is a staunch pointer, and a good retriever to boot.

Another noteworthy European gun dog is the German shorthaired pointer. The German shorthair is far more popular than its wirehaired relative. The shorthair is a top-notch bird dog that can learn to handle a variety of game. Its big virtue in the eyes of many hunters is that it tends to range closer to the gun than the English pointer.

There is little doubt that the German shorthair is a fine producer. It is particularly favored on many shooting preserves, where a dog must not only be able to point, but also to retrieve.

The vizsla is an attractive dog with a smooth, honey-colored coat. It was developed as a gun dog on the game-rich plains of Hungary. It has also adapted well to this continent. The vizsla can be trained to handle a variety of upland game and is a proficient retriever. Most vizslas are somewhat closer ranging than German shorthairs, but in other ways their method of working is similar.

The Brittany spaniel is another of the "Continental" types. This dog should probably have been called the Brittany setter, because unlike the other spaniels, the Brittany is a pointing and not a flushing dog. The Brittany is a reliable dog in heavy brush because it can slither under obstacles that bigger dogs would have to crash through. It is a good grouse and woodcock dog.

Some strains of Brittanys are close ranging, but field-trial bloodlines generally are not. Many Brittanys are fairly big going, just as wide ranging as some strains of the German

Gun Dogs for Upland Game

Weimaraners frozen in immobility. The case for these dogs was originally so overstated that no dog could live up to it and weimaraners soon fell into disfavor. As the picture shows, however, well-trained dogs of this breed not only can find birds, but are also staunch and deadly serious on the point. Photo: Leonard Lee Rue III.

shorthair. This has ruined them in the eyes of many hunters.

The Brittany is a sensitive dog that needs to be trained with a light hand. Some Brittanys are very good retrievers. In general, Brittanys are fine, all-around upland game dogs and can learn to hunt most birds.

Another upland bird dog that has appeared on the American hunting scene is the weimaraner. This breed came into great demand in the late 1940s, and was given much publicity as a talented superdog. The weimaraner did not live up to all its expectations, but the claims made for the dog were more than any breed could live up to.

The weimaraner is a large, lean, short-haired dog—striking in appearance. It weighs 75 to 80 pounds and stands some 26 inches at the withers. In the hands of an able trainer this breed has proven capable in the upland field. But it does have a tendency to be a bit of a plodder, which some upland bird dog fanciers don't care for.

Dogs for Flushing and Retrieving

Dogs that find game and scare it up, then retrieve it, are called flushers. For birds that have a tendency to run ahead of the hunter, flushers can be of great assistance. Dogs of this type may not require the extensive training of the pointers and setters. They often hunt by body scent, and with sufficient training will do so at a pace that allows the hunter to stay within shooting range.

The best known flushing breed is the cocker spaniel, a small dog with a warm disposition—good as a pet. The disadvantage of the cocker is that it has been overbred so thoroughly that one of good field stock is now very hard to find.

A somewhat larger dog than the cocker (40 pounds as opposed to the cocker's 25 or 30) is the springer spaniel. With the increase in the pheasant population and the consequent increase in hunters afield for this bird, the springer spaniel has come into its own. The springer takes to hunting the ringneck with a thoroughness and drive that leaves little to be desired in an upland bird dog.

Unfortunately, spaniels have long hair that catches burrs, but they work well in heavy grass and shintangle, and hunt both by body scent and by trailing.

One fine but relatively little known flushing dog is the American water spaniel. Bred as a small retriever to work out of boats, the American water spaniel is really a capable little all-around gun dog. It is brown in color and, unlike the other spaniels, has a long tail. It is a mild dog that hunts close and is a very capable retriever. It is a particularly good bet for a hunter who cannot keep up to the energetic zip of the springer spaniel. The American water spaniel can do a good job on ruffed grouse, woodcock, pheasants, and ducks, retrieving

Gun Dogs for Upland Game

from small ponds and marshes. It deserves to be better known and more popular than it is.

On the ringneck too, there is another dog that is able, willing, and strong—the Labrador retriever. Introduced largely as a dog for waterfowl, the Lab has proven itself capable on upland game as well. The Lab is stocky, strong of build, and has a stamina that allows it to keep on going almost effortlessly well into the day. Its size—24 inches at the withers and 60 to 75 pounds—rules it out as a house dog in cramped quarters.

In color, most Labrador retrievers are black. But some wear a pure blond-tan or rarely a chocolate brown coat. The hair is short. The Labrador is a spectacular water dog, but many up-

One of the best breeds for all-around hunting is the golden retriever, which combines handsomeness and intelligence with an ability to function with distinction both as water dog and upland game dog.
Photo: Leonard Lee Rue III.

THE SHOTGUN

Dog—and bird—expert John R. Falk congratulates a springer spaniel
on a job well done. Dogs are quick to respond to a pat and a word
of praise. Photo: Leonard Lee Rue III.

land hunters rate it as tops for its steady, unfaltering performance in the uplands as well.

Another retriever is the Chesapeake. Like the former, the Chesapeake is noted for its ability to retrieve waterfowl. At the same time it can work out as a dog for flushing upland game. The Chesapeake is a fairly stocky dog—65 to 70 pounds in weight and standing a good 2 feet high at the shoulder. In

Gun Dogs for Upland Game

color, the Chesapeake is usually a solid tan or brown. Both the Labrador and the Chesapeake are able hunters, and when chosen from good bloodlines make able upland-hunting companions as well as dogs worth having around the home. They are both mild tempered and patient.

Still another retriever breed is the golden—a beautiful dog that may be seriously impaired for hunting because it has become the darling of show dog people. The golden retriever has a soft temperament and a tractable attitude. It is probably an even better bet for upland hunting than the Labrador.

The Right Dog

With many hunters, a good dog is essential for success in the field. Discerning hunters will go to some lengths to find a dog that measure up to what a good hunting dog should be. It's always wise to pick one that fits both the hunter's housing accommodations and field requirements.

When buying a pup, always pick a scion of good hunting stock. Select a puppy that seems to be eager, lively, intent, and healthy. Train and treat it well. Encourage it. After a successful performance let it know your appreciation with words of praise.

The right dog will go far towards making the hunting day considerably more enjoyable.

14

The Bird Hunter's Wardrobe

The weather during the bird season can be chilly on some days and fairly mild on others, so clothing must be chosen accordingly. I have hunted grouse and also woodcock when snow was on the ground, while on other occasions the weather was as warm as summer. Thus a good investment in an outer garment is a loose-fitting coat of moderate weight under which a woolen shirt can be added if necessary.

Underwear can be either the conventional cotton shirt-and-shorts, or, where the hunting is on the colder side, the long-legged underdrawers and the long-sleeved cotton T-shirt. The two-piece thermal-knit cotton undergarment is usually too warm for this season, but it can be worn if the weather turns cold.

Woolen undergarments for this time of year are really unnecessary. During the upland season the hunter is fairly active and is usually able to keep comfortable with medium-weight garments, except during midday when he is sitting down and relaxing. An extra sweater or shirt can be carried against such occasions and is well worth having for emergency wear.

For early season upland hunting, the hard-finished cotton shirt fills the bill nicely. If the weather is on the coolish side you can wear a woolen shirt over it. Generous patch pockets will come in handy on either shirt for the small items the hunter likes to carry with him.

Hunting pants should be selected with care, as they take a beating when you're tramping through brush and brambles. Much of the time you will encounter snags, thistles, burrs, briars, and brush, all of which dictates wearing pants that are tough and briar-resistant. Wool is not the answer.

A fabric such as duck and durable cotton poplin with a hard finish and tough weave will serve admirably for bird-hunting trousers. Pants without cuffs, so they do not pick up dirt and trash, are recommended. Get them roomy enough so they fit loosely. Also, make sure they have deep and roomy pockets to hold those small items such as knife, keys, and matchbox. "Lightweight but durable" is the way to describe the best in outdoor trousers.

Some hunters want the cuffs tucked inside the boot top; others want them outside. It's all a matter of personal taste and makes little difference. For color, marsh brown is recommended in that it usually blends with the autumn scenery and has a certain camouflaging effect.

The bird hunter's footgear should be light and comfortable, to keep him going all day long with no bothersome sore feet or blisters ensuing. Be selective here, for there are several brands of good boots on the market to choose from. Avoid high-topped footgear unless hunting in snake-infested country.

One of the best choices in footgear is the "Birdshooter," a light, sturdy, low-topped Vibram-soled boot with eyelets for lacing near the bottom and lace "speed" hooks at the top. This 8-inch-high leather boot has uppers of water-repellent, oil-tanned leather, a leather lined vamp, and a moccasin toe. The best have low heels with an up-sloping front edge, so the wearer does not hook his heel into rocks, sticks, logs, and other such projections. A boot like this need not be absolutely waterproof, but it can be made pretty much so with one of the waterproofing products on the market.

The size should be ample so that one pair of cotton socks can be worn along with a pair of light woolen socks over them, and still accommodate any swelling of the feet that may result from a day's walking. Make sure boots fit well at the shop: not too tight, not too loose. Then break them in gradually on short trips.

There are still a few upland gunners who prefer the Indian type of moccasin. One make has a one-piece vamp construction with an additional layer of leather added to the sole, giving the wearer two thick layers of leather to walk on. Another style provides heavy-duty moccasins that are hand sewn, the leather on the sides and bottom being 3/16 inch thick and affording long wear. For getting around in the uplands this type of footgear is light, but needless to say, not everybody can wear moccasins. They do, however, have unique styling and many hunters consider them both practical and comfortable.

Leather footgear fits most conditions when the weather is dry, but there are also occasions where the all-rubber boot or the rubber-and-leather boot is a good investment. If the weather

When bird hunting in cold weather, a felt-lined boot—such as this one from L. L. Bean—can help ensure that the excursion is pleasant rather than a misery. Photo: L. L. Bean.

is really wet you will find the all-rubber boot just what you need to keep the feet and legs dry. This boot allows you to cut through small streams and puddles when after such game as pheasants. There are times, too, when you may want to hunt grouse or woodcock in the damp of the early morning, in which case the rubber boot is a good choice while the dew is still heavy on the grass; to be exchanged for the leather boot after the sun dries things out.

If you happen to be a deer as well as an upland-bird hunter, you may have solved the problem of wet-weather hunting footgear with the rubber-bottom, leather-top boot that is so useful later in the season. The L. L. Bean model, for instance, is light and comfortable and can be made very warm later in the year by wearing all-wool socks with it. For early morning upland hunting, when the grass is still wet or when there's moisture in the air, you can do yourself a great favor by wearing this combination.

These boots are made for wading shallow creeks or stepping in puddles along the way, as well as for hunting damp, slushy, or snow-covered terrain. Wear the boots all day if the weather is on the damp side. But if the sun comes up shining and the terrain dries out, you may want to change to an all-leather boot.

Any boot you select, whether leather, rubber, or rubber-leather, should lace snugly to keep out seeds, chaff, grass, and other material that tends to get in through the top. Be sure the soles have a snug grip so that you do not slip and slide.

The peaked canvas or duck-hunting cap is a good piece of headgear for the bird hunter. It is lightweight and waterproof and its broad brim provides good shade for the eyes on bright, sunny days. Should the cap become too warm, it is also small enough to be folded and thrust into the coat pocket. On the other hand, many an upland hunter will prefer a light felt hat for the reason that it is usually well broken in, is soft, comfortable, and better than most caps for shading the eyes as well as turning off rain.

In shirt-sleeve hunting weather, another "must" garment for many hunters is a game vest. Choose one that has ample pockets for ammunition and a roomy, rubberized game bag in the back. These come in many colors nowadays—greens, browns, camouflage, and even blaze orange. The latter is particularly favored by grouse and woodcock hunters because it can readily be seen even in dense cover.

The best game vests are those on which the game pockets can be loaded from the front as well as the rear. Never choose a game vest on which the game bag cannot be detached or unsnapped fully for cleaning.

When the weather turns chilly, wool is the hunter's best friend. A shirt such as this one will work wonders in keeping you comfortable in the field. Photo: L. L. Bean.

While wool provides warmth, it is not a great protector against wetness. A parka, such as this, worn over wool, will do much to keep a hunter comfortable in rain or snow. Photo: L. L. Bean.

The Bird Hunter's Wardrobe

For real warm-weather hunting, such as is frequently encountered on a dove or quail hunt in the South or Southwest, there are game vests on which the panels over the shoulders and back are made of a loose-knit, netlike material. In hot weather, these are a real boon.

In cooler weather, a light jacket of water-repellent fabric makes a convenient outer garment. A canvas coat, or one of lightweight duck, takes first place in this category and serves well. This type of coat cuts off the wind and rain, and if ample—which it should be—will give freedom of movement as well as allow enough room for wearing a woolen shirt underneath.

Make sure the coat you select is provided with pockets for carrying bagged birds, as well as your shells and lunch.

The canvas hunting coat sheds water well and also allows body vapor to seep through the fabric. With collar and wristbands of softer material, it fits well at all points and will last almost indefinitely.

An alternative for upland hunting in colder weather is the plaid woolen cruiser, also cut to ample proportions. It should be fingertip in length, warm, and soft to the touch. It should also have plenty of room about the hips. Although not waterproof, it should be water repellent to a degree and quick drying. Toward the end of the upland season, when the days become chill, this jacket is well worth wearing. It sheds rain or snow and is just what the active man at this time of year will find to his liking. This cruiser may not have any game pocket, but instead the hunter can easily carry a small knapsack for game, shells, lunch, and the like.

A light plastic raincoat that folds into a small bundle is well worth its low price as an extra garment to carry in the field. It will keep you really dry early in the morning, especially, when grass and brush are wet. It also affords protection if a sudden shower springs up.

Be dressed in the field to fit the day and hunting conditions at all times, and you'll come through with comfort and ease.

15

Shotgun Safety

Shotgun safety is really a matter of common sense. Unfortunately, there are some hunters who seem to lack this commodity. Any kind of hunting can be dangerous if you are careless with firearms. The man who values his privilege to be out in the field with gun and dog will do his best to handle his sporting arms with caution and consideration, and at all times with an eye to the safety of his fellows as well as himself.

The basis for sportsmanship in woods and field is proper regard for hunting partners and the land on which you are hunting, as well as the careful use and handling of the firearm you are carrying. You will always have to be vigilant and considerate, but if you train yourself from the beginning, safety will come as second nature. Whether you are hunting with a shotgun, a .22 rimfire, or a high-powered big-game rifle, you are handling a lethal weapon. If you always remember to keep it pointed away from others, you should never do harm to anyone.

Understand how your firearm functions. Load it on entering the field; unload it when the hunting trip is over. Thoroughly.

Accidents have happened too often because of the forgotten shell in the magazine. If you make sure that all shells are removed from the magazine and chambers when the hunting day is at an end, your gun will be safe. Until it's reloaded.

Don't take chances on your target. When there's a noise or disturbance in the brush, for instance, determine definitely that it's a game bird or animal you've heard and not just some unknown object that you don't want to shoot. It is unsafe to be overanxious to bag your quarry. Make sure it's legal game— whether four-footed or feathered—before pressing the trigger. To fire first and then determine what you've shot at is a practice that leads to shooting accidents.

Every time a hunter picks up a gun he should assume responsibility for it. That means in camp, in the car, or in the field.

One of the cardinal rules of gun safety is to treat every gun with the respect due to a loaded gun. Any companion who fails to comply with this rule had best be left at home. Your tried-and-true hunting partner will always play safe with firearms; that is why he is your trusted companion. You can always rely on his conduct in the field.

In wilderness areas of the Northwestern States, New England, and even Wisconsin, Minnesota, northern Michigan, and Canada, grouse—both blue and ruffed—are hunted by cruising forest roads with an automobile. This method of hunting (if it can be called hunting) causes many gun accidents every year. Why? Because some of the "hunters" carry loaded guns in their cars in order to get off a quick shot if they see a bird. Carrying a loaded firearm in a vehicle is, of course, illegal, although in some states and Canadian provinces a hunter can have shells in the magazine. Firearms in cars should be carried empty and loaded only after you have stepped out of the vehicle and are ready for the shot.

There was a time when an ambitious hunter stood on the front bumper of his car and, with a nonhunter driving, picked off the birds he saw along the logging road. This method of bagging game is now illegal everywhere. Thank God for that.

THE SHOTGUN

Its sporting ethics were low. When road hunting today, the proper procedure is to bring the car to a stop when a bird is spotted. You then should step out of the car, load your gun outside, and then try to bag the bird. You are certainly hand-icapped in this way, but it does point up that for spirited and healthy hunting, it's best to try to bag game on foot and give the sport of bird hunting the respect it deserves. You may not fare so well where the game is wary, but you'll enjoy the hunt much more.

It is, after all, a great satisfaction to get out into the autumn field and forest and travel with gun in hand. At such times, you will find yourself looking over the woods and cover with a freshly appreciative eye. Not only will you free yourself from the entanglements of the workaday world, but you can see what game you can encounter and bring to bag. It is not even so much the amount of game you get that will be your reward. It is the sport of the thing—getting away from the tensions of everyday life and enjoying yourself in a different world.

Of course, there will be the problem of competing with the swift and elusive game encountered. Where will the next bird show up? What kind of shot will you be able to get this time? How much lead do you want on this quick-flying bird? But that's part of the challenge. The aware hunter will do his best to make a good showing for himself, but will not devote him-self solely to the practice of bagging as much game as he can. With an eye to the future, he will realize that there is only so much game available, and that he must be farsighted enough to make it last.

Other years for hunting must be kept in mind. The more a man hunts and the more lessons he learns about hunting, the more he comes to realize the true issue of conservation: Leave some for the other fellow and for seed.

Hunting has had a great attraction for ages, and will have that allurement as long as there is game in the field. There is no financial gain at stake—the day of the market gunner is passed. But the sport of hunting is an enjoyable one, and if properly pursued is here to stay.

Shotgun Safety

PART TWO

THE RIFLE

16

Hunting the Uplands with Rifle

When a hunter takes his big-game rifle off the gun rack or out of the closet you can be almost certain as to what animal he plans to hunt—deer. I'm sure that more man-days are spent deer hunting in any one year than in hunting all other big game in twenty years. Likewise, I'm sure that more center-fire ammunition is expended on deer in one year than on all other big game in twenty years. And I'd bet my favorite deer rifle that more big-game rifles are bought each year with deer hunting in mind than for varmint hunting or any big game other than deer.

This brings us to a subject that has caused more arguments in deer camps than religion and politics combined: What is the best deer rifle. In choosing that rifle, the hunter has two major factors to consider—the best caliber, and the type of action he prefers. There are four popular types of actions on the market: the lever action, the slide, the semiautomatic, and the bolt action.

The Lever Action

The lever action is the oldest type of repeating rifle. It is one of the most popular types, particularly among deer hunters of the Eastern forests. This is partially due to its reliability, as well as that the lever-action rifle is light, handy, and allows fast successive shots. It can be used by both right- or left-handed shooters. That it has been around for over a century has ingrained it in the minds of many hunters.

There are two basic types of lever actions. The older types, such as the Winchester 94, the Marlin 336, and the Mossberg 472, have exposed hammers, tubular magazines under the barrel, and are generally chambered for less intense cartridges, such as the fine old .30-30 or the relatively new .444 Marlin Magnum. Dixie and Navy Arms also make replicas of early Winchester lever actions in .44-40, .38 Special, and .44 Magnum cartridges.

The newer type of lever action, such as the Savage 99 and the Winchester 88, have stronger actions and clip magazines. They shoot modern, high-intensity cartridges such as the .308 and .243 Winchester and the .300 Savage. The Browning lever action is a sort of hybrid between the other types of lever actions. It has an exposed hammer like the Winchester 94 or the Marlin 336, but a clip-type box magazine. This very strong action is chambered for the .243, .308, and .358 Winchester cartridges.

The Slide Action

The slide, or pump, rifle is fast and handy, especially useful where fast successive shots are frequently needed. The slide-action rifles have their following, but they are not as popular as the bolt action or the lever. Slide-action rifles have never achieved the popularity of the pump shotgun. Slide-action big-game rifles are made by Remington and Savage.

The Winchester Model 94 lever-action rifle is the most popular deer rifle ever marketed anywhere in the world. Photo: Winchester-Western.

The Ruger Number One Light Sporter weighs but 7¼ pounds and is available in several popular deer-hunting chamberings. As it is a single-shot rifle, it is recommended only for the hunter with demonstrated confidence in his marksmanship. Photo: Sturm Ruger and Co.

Pump rifles are chambered for cartridges from the old .30-30 to the .30-06. Like the lever action, the slide action can be used by left- or right-handed shooters.

The Semiautomatic

The semiautomatic rifle is at least as popular as the pump. Modern semiautomatics are fairly light and reliable; they are preferred by hunters who want a second or third shot quickly. Semiautomatic rifles have slightly softer recoil than other actions with rifles of the same weight and chambered for the same cartridge. This is due to some of the gas from the powder being used to "power" the action.

In big-game cartridges, semiautomatics are made by Remington, Ruger, Harrington and Richardson, and Browning. They can be had in a variety of calibers from .270 Winchester to .44 Magnum, and even in the .300 Winchester Magnum.

Hunting the Uplands with Rifle

One of the great bolt-action rifles of all time, the Winchester Model 70 has proven its worth many times over to deer hunters as well as those after other kinds of game. Photo: Winchester-Western.

The Winchester Model 670, a more economical version of the company's Model 70, comes equipped with a 4X Weaver scope. Photo: Winchester-Western.

The Bolt Action

Bolt-action rifles are generally considered to be simpler and more rugged and foolproof than the lever actions. They can also take the stronger pressures of high-intensity cartridges. The bolt-action rifle is the most accurate of all rifles, but successive shots cannot be fired as rapidly as with other actions.

The bolt action is made in a variety of styles, weights, and barrel lengths and is chambered for a greater variety of cartridges than any other rifle, from the .22 Hornet to the ponderous .460 Weatherby elephant rifle.

Winchester, Remington, Ruger, Savage, Weatherby, and a host of fine European firearms manufacturers all make bolt-action rifles. Bolt actions are also made by many custom gunmakers. Most of these are modified Mauser 98 types. Other types of bolt actions which do not use the Mauser system are the Mannlicher, the Shultz and Larsen, the new Colt Sauer, and the new Mauser 66.

The Best Action

There is really no such thing as a best action. It all depends on what you prefer and what you're used to. A hunter who uses a pump shotgun on game birds may well prefer a pump rifle for deer because he's used to the action. A hunter who uses a semiauto shotgun may prefer a semiautomatic rifle because it operates the same way. It also has the safety catch in the same location and softer recoil.

Generally speaking, bolt actions are more accurate than the other types. By this I don't mean that off-the-counter bolt-action rifles will be significantly more accurate than equivalent pumps or semiautomatics. But the bolt action does have the capacity to become more accurate once it is tuned up by a knowledgeable rifleman or gunsmith.

My advice to any deer hunter is to pick the rifle of the action type he is most comfortable hunting with. This is the first step in acquiring confidence in a gun. Any of the four popular actions make good deer rifles.

Choosing the Caliber

Deer have been shot with everything from a .22 Long Rifle to some of the ponderous cartridges designed for dangerous African game. To a large degree, the caliber and the cartridge play second fiddle in the actual death of the animal. Bullet placement—the actual placement of the shot—is far more important. There are deer hunters around who don't regard the .30-30 as an adequate deer cartridge. This is foolish. The .30-30 has killed more deer than any cartridge ever designed.

Another fallacy is that modern deer hunters need more powerful, harder-hitting cartridges because they shoot more deer on the run and because they have to take any shot they can.

There may be some truth to this, in that most deer, especially

Hunting the Uplands with Rifle

whitetails, are shot on the run. But that's only because most of us aren't the woodsmen our forefathers were, and we cannot surprise a browsing or bedded deer as they were able to. Also, there are more hunters in the woods now. This in itself keeps the deer moving and jittery. There is little doubt that deer today are wiser and warier than those of yesteryear. That may be another reason why modern hunters seldom get standing shots.

But to suggest that a hunter can compensate for bad bullet placement and bad shooting by using a more powerful cartridge is the height of irresponsibility. That kind of statement only encourages deer hunters to take poor shots, hoping that the XYZ Magnum will compensate for poor shooting and poorly placed shots. A gut-shot deer, whether shot with a .30-30 or a .375 Holland and Holland Magnum, is still a gut-shot deer. It is going to travel a long way before dying. The .375 H & H Magnum is not going to kill a deer any quicker than a .30-30. If a deer hunter makes a bum shot and breaks a deer's front leg, what difference does it make what caliber or cartridge the hunter used. It is totally irrelevant as to how the leg was broken.

Much has been written about the killing efficiency, the so-called "shock effect" of the modern expanding bullet, particularly those driven at high velocity from some of the more modern cartridges. Frankly, my opinion is that shock effect alone is incapable of killing big-game animals, even big-game animals as small as deer.

There is only one way to get a quick, humane kill on a deer (or any animal), and that is by hitting the animal in the vital organs. Animals are quickly killed by hits that destroy or disrupt such vital organs as the heart or the lungs. Brain shots or even those that sever the spinal cord in the neck kill even faster, because they disrupt the central nervous system.

Choosing the best caliber for a deer rifle is beset with problems. The reason, of course, is that there is no best caliber under all conditions that deer are hunted. On the other hand, there are a number of calibers that are quite suitable for deer in the Eastern woods or the Western foothills.

Outdoor writers have been fond of dividing requirements for deer rifles into "rifles for the Western deer" and "rifles for whitetails." This is fine. It makes interesting reading for gun buffs and a few dollars for gun writers. But when reading such articles, one must know how to separate the wheat from the chaff.

For example, the articles on rifles for Western deer usually describe only the best calibers for mule deer, which are hunted in semiopen country. The articles on the best rifles for whitetails on the other hand always describe the best calibers for deer hunting in the thick Eastern woods. The problem, of course, is that not all Western deer are hunted in semiopen terrain. Blacktails are deer of thick forests, and any rifle that is a good choice for Eastern whitetails will be a good bet for Pacific blacktails.

On the other hand, the good deer rifle for the Eastern woods may be far from ideal for the little Coues whitetail found in the open brush and scrub country of the Southwest. The ideal rifle for the Coues whitetail would be a good bet for mule deer as well.

A deer hunter, then, should pay close attention to the type of bullet available—particularly bullet weight—when considering the merits of one caliber over another. In some ways, the bullet weight is more important than the actual caliber of the bullet.

It is generally acknowledged that deer rifles for the woods should fire a relatively heavy bullet, or one of high sectional density, at moderate velocity. This type of bullet is less likely to deflect and ricochet off target if it hits a twig or branch. The bullet should be roundnosed, not pointed, for much the same reason.

On the other hand, deer rifles for open, mule-deer country should fire a bullet at fairly high velocity so that its trajectory is fairly flat—the flatter the better. The reason, of course, is that

Hunting the Uplands with Rifle

mule deer are generally shot at greater ranges than whitetails in the brush. Certainly the potential for long shots frequently arises. A bullet that flies with a flat trajectory makes hitting more certain.

All this dictates bullets of lighter weight because they can be driven faster, and bullets with pointed tips, because of their ballistic coefficient in meeting air resistance.

On the basis of these criteria, we can divide calibers and bullet weights into two groups: one most suitable for forest deer hunting; the other for open hunting in mountain foothills. From this list, one can easily see that there are a number of cartridges that can be used for both types of hunting. The old .30-06 or the newer .308 Winchester are good examples. With 150-grain pointed bullets, both cartridges are suitable for mule-deer hunting. But when loaded with 180-grain, round-nosed slugs, they are favored by many Eastern woods deer hunters or hunters after blacktails in the evergreen forests of the Pacific coast.

DEER CARTRIDGES FOR WOODS HUNTING

Cartridge	Bullet weight in grains
.270 Winchester	150
.280 Remington	165
7 × 57 mm	175
.30-30 Winchester	150
.30-30 Winchester	170
.30-06	180
.308 Winchester	180
.303 British	180
.32 Winchester Special	180
8 × 57 mm	170
.35 Remington	200
.358 Winchester	200
.350 Remington Magnum	200
.44 Remington Magnum	240
.444 Marlin	240
.45-70	405

Cartridge	Bullet weight in grains
.243 Winchester	100
.244 Remington	90
6 mm Remington	100
.240 Weatherby	100
.25-06	100
.25-06	117
.250-3000 Savage	100
.257 Roberts	100
.257 Weatherby	100
.257 Weatherby	117
.264 Winchester	140
6.5 mm Remington Magnum	120
.270 Winchester	130
.280 Remington	150
.284 Winchester	150
7 × 57 mm	139
7 mm Remington Magnum	150
.30-06	150
.300 Savage	150
.300 Winchester Magnum	150
.300 Winchester Magnum	180
.300 Weatherby Magnum	150
.300 Weatherby Magnum	180
.300 Holland and Holland Magnum	150
.300 Holland and Holland Magnum	180
.308 Winchester	150
.303 British	150

Rifle Sights

To shoot accurately, a rifle must be equipped with good sights. There are three types of sights commonly used on rifles: the open sight, the apterure sight, and the scope sight.

The open sight is the most common sight on rifles. It consists

Hunting the Uplands with Rifle

of a bead or post for the front sight and a notched piece of metal for the rear. Most rifles from the factory come equipped with open sights. Many hunters prefer this sight because they are used to it and feel comfortable with it. The biggest objection to the open sight is that it demands focusing the eye on three things at once: the rear sight, the front sight, and the target. A young shooter with nimble eyes can make this adjustment fairly well, but the person with older eyes may have trouble lining up the sights for a fast and accurate shot. The open sight is also apt to appear fuzzy under certain light conditions and may cause a person to overshoot. Another objection to open sights is that there is a tendency for the shooter not to get his eye down on the sight properly. This also causes him to overshoot.

One of the best open sights is the shallow u with a white line down the center, as is found on the Savage .300. Some of the poorest are the buckhorn-type rear sights, which block the view of the target.

The aperture or peep sight is considered superior to the open sight since the sighting comes up quicker and easier once a shooter is used to it. You look through the peep, not at it. The eye automatically centers on the front sight. When using the peep, one can see the entire deer in the circular field of the sight. The secret to using a peep sight is to have a big aperture. It is best to remove the disc aperture in the peep and discard it. This leaves the large screwhole to aim through, offering the shooter a wider field of view and a better chance to make a fast shot. The fine disc aperture should only be used for target shooting.

The main objection to the peep sight is that the recoil on the big-game rifle may place it too close to the eye and jam it back when firing. The peep sight, however, is more accurate than the open sight. It also has the advantage of micrometer adjustments for both elevation and windage, which makes sighting in the rifle much easier.

With either open and peep sight, the front bead must stand

out so that it is seen quickly and easily. Some hunters who do their shooting in Eastern cover prefer an ivory bead, but ivory is not for the man who will do his hunting against a snowy background. In the latter case, among the best colors are red and gold, with red preferred.

The telescopic or scope sight is the best for almost any hunting, especially for deer. Its only drawback is that it adds more weight to the rifle. The scope enables the hunter to see and hit game that he might otherwise miss. It also permits him to pick out and examine game even through brush, and determine the sex and trophy value of the animal. For persons with failing eyesight, the scope sight is a boon and a blessing.

For deer hunting in brushy country, I recommend a 2½- or 2¾x scope which offers a wide field of view and good aiming in the process. Some hunters prefer the 4x scope for all-around deer hunting, but it does not equal the 2¾x for hunting deer in brushy cover. The 2¾x offers a much wider field of view, which is the key to getting on the deer fast. In Eastern hunting, the deer usually appears at close range and is fast moving. The shot must be a quick snap or none at all.

The best reticles for scope sights for the Eastern woods are a coarse cross hair or a large dot. But some hunters still prefer the post.

Another scope sight that is becoming popular is the variable scope, which can be adjusted to several ranges of power. The most popular variables are the 1.5x-4x and the 3x-9x. The variable is best used with cross hairs, for a dot or post reticle tends to get larger as the power is increased. Left at the lowest power, the variable scope is effective for brushy-cover deer shooting. But if this is all a hunter will use it for, then there's no need for a variable scope. The 2¾x is lighter in weight and cheaper to buy.

The variable power scope is the best bet for all-around big-game rifles used for the Eastern woods or the foothills country of the West, or even for antelope in the open plains. For mule-deer hunting in the Western hills, a 4x scope with medium

Hunting the Uplands with Rifle

cross hairs is an excellent choice. There may be some hunters who prefer 6x scopes, but 4x are more popular.

While the scope is a bit slower on sighting, it does make for better shooting, assuring more clean kills. Another advantage of the scope is that it "gathers light." A hunter with a scope-sighted rifle can shoot earlier at dawn and later at dusk because he can see the game through the scope. This can be an important edge, because deer move about most at dusk and dawn.

For many hunters, a combination of the open factory sights along with a swing-away scope, or quick detachable scope mounts, is an ideal solution. Should the scope sight become fogged or prove too slow for close-range shooting, it can be flipped over or detached to allow use of the open sight. However, the best scopes are now water and moisture proof. Several firms, in fact, guarantee that their scopes are absolutely fog and moisture proof. There is also a possibility that the lense on any scope may become covered with water, but this can quickly be remedied by the wipe of a thumb.

Sling Swivels

Sling swivels are a useful item on any deer rifle. They should be of the quick-detachable kind so that the sling can be removed during the actual hunt, because swivels can rattle. The time when a sling is useful is when you've bagged your buck and are now faced with the task of dragging him back to camp. For that, you need two hands.

The Shotgun as a "Deer Rifle"

In many parts of the densely settled East, deer hunters are not allowed to use rifles for deer hunting. They must use either rifled slugs or buckshot. (In some states buckshot is also banned because it is not as efficient.)

THE RIFLE

There is little doubt that the 12-gauge shotgun with 1 ounce of slugs with a diameter of .729 inches is the most lethal. A 16-gauge slug is also quite good, but most hunting authorities do not recommend slugs any smaller. The small .410 slugs should even be banned.

Although most shotgun deer hunters use the same shotgun they use for bird shooting, this is not the best idea. A shotgun has no rear sight, and without this it's hard to shoot slugs accurately. Double-barreled shotguns—side-by-sides and over-unders—are even worse. A hunter who hunts deer regularly in a shotguns only area is best advised to get a special slug gun with good sights. For a hunter who hunts with a pump or semiautomatic shotgun, that is relatively easy. All he has to do is purchase a special slug barrel with rear sights. Most manufacturers of pump and semiautomatic shotguns make them.

Another possibility is to buy a second-hand gun—an inexpensive bolt action is fine—and have a gunsmith mount a rear sight on it. An open or aperture sight, or even a scope, can be mounted on a shotgun.

You could, if you wish, even mount a scope sight on a quick-detachable side mount on your semiauto or pump bird gun, and then take the sight or scope off during the bird season. The problem is that the base for the aperture sight or scope mount remains on the receiver of the shotgun, somewhat spoiling its sleek lines. But there are some pragmatic hunters who don't mind.

With good sights, a shotgun with slugs retains enough accuracy for deer hunting up to about 100 yards. Most whitetails are shot at ranges less than that.

In the Southern swamps, deer are shot with buckshot. The ranges are short and the deer move quickly, making the shotgun with buckshot a logical choice for such hunting. The best buckshot is probably 0 or No. 1 because it is abundant enough to give good dense patterns. Buckshot smaller than No. 2 should not be used on deer.

Hunting the Uplands with Rifle

The best gauge is the 12, but a 16 can also be used. The new Federal 3-inch Magnum with No. 2 buckshot even brings the 20 gauge up to the level of the 16.

Buckshot is constantly lethal only to about 40 yards, with perhaps the 12-gauge 3-inch Magnum in 00 buck having a range of 50 yards. Beyond this, shooting at deer with buckshot is chancy. The risk of crippling is high. Anyone hunting deer with buckshot should pattern his shotgun to find a brand and load that delivers good, dense patterns. Then stick with that brand and load.

Care of the Rifle

One consideration about purchasing and owning a good rifle is that it will last a lifetime with proper attention. It won't wear out under normal usage, and if given reasonable care will come through any hunt in fine shape. Toward this end, the rifle should be thoroughly cleaned when returning from the field. Prepare for this job by obtaining a suitable cleaning kit from a sporting-goods store. The kit should contain a metal cleaning rod (either solid or jointed), gun grease, gun solvent, and cleaning patches.

The solid rod is superior to the jointed one, but is more cumbersome. Most hunters use jointed rods that come in two or three pieces and have two or three interchangeable tips (one with a cleaning brush) and a revolving handle.

Flannel patches for swabbing are preferred. These are durable and do a thorough cleaning job. Hoppe's Gun Cleaning Pack has been on the market for years and contains everything necessary to keep your firearm rust-free and clean. It contains gun grease, nitro powder solvent, and cleaning patches.

To clean a rifle, first saturate a patch with solvent on a cleaning rod and work back and forth in the bore until the bore is well cleaned. Then wipe with a fresh patch. Repeat this until the bore is bright and the cleaning patch shows no stains.

THE RIFLE

Many shooters keep their barrels as clean as a whistle and think they've finished the job. Unless they pay some attention to the chamber, however, they're not doing justice to the firearm. Use a wire brush or put a large piece of flannel on the end of the cleaning rod and clean that chamber thoroughly. In this way, when you want to fire your rifle, you can be certain it will be dependable.

If you're putting the gun away for a while, coat the bore with gun grease to preserve it. For a good job here, polish the outside of the barrel thoroughly with a clean flannel rag and coat it with a thin layer of oil.

If the stock has taken on a dull luster, this can be restored to normal by a rubdown with boiled linseed oil.

Check the gun as a whole for any parts that may have come loose or need replacing. If the gun is stored in its case, leave the case partly open so that moisture can escape. Moisture from condensation during storage is often the cause of rusting.

Before using the rifle on the next hunting trip, make sure the grease is removed and that all parts are in prime condition. This should be done well in advance of the deer season—not a day or two before. That way, if something is amiss, a gunsmith still has time to fix it.

17

Hunting
Upland Deer

Deer are the bread and butter of American big-game hunting. Moose, elk, the various species of sheep, bear, mountain goat, caribou, and even pronghorn antelope may all be more glamorous trophies to bag, but a hunt for any one of these species is beyond the family budget of many hunters. Almost anyone, however, can afford to go on a deer hunt. Every state in the Union has a deer season. Indeed, deer can be hunted within a couple of hours drive of any of our large cities.

One reason why deer hunting is so popular is that the animal is prolific and adaptable. It is found throughout the United States, including Hawaii, and in much of Canada. Deer can be hunted by anyone—young and old alike—who knows how to handle a rifle, shotgun, or even a bow and arrow. Although deer is big game, you don't have to mount an expedition to go after it. You have only to know how to handle your gun, to learn something about the habits of your quarry, and to get out into deer country. With a little luck, you'll come home with some delicious venison and memories for years to come.

The deer that are hunted in North America fall into two broad categories—whitetail deer and mule deer. Whitetails are more populous and widespread, being found in all the contiguous states except portions of Washington, Oregon, Idaho, California, Nevada, Utah, Colorado, and Arizona. Mule deer, including the black-tailed subspecies, is the other major species of deer. However, except for parts of Minnesota and Iowa, it is hardly found east of the Mississippi River. The blacktail race ranges from northern California right up to the coastal evergreen forests into southern Alaska, where it is called the Sitka deer.

Mule deer, on the other hand, are found in the more open forests or rolling hills on the eastern slopes of the Rockies, from Mexico north to British Columbia and east to Minnesota. The most sought-after mule deer are the Rocky Mountain vari-

Once snow is on the ground, the successful hunter may profit from the use of a snowmobile to get his deer back home or to camp. Photo: Wisconsin Conservation Department.

Hunting Upland Deer

Deer abound
almost
everywhere and
in all manner of
conditions. Here
an early season
hunter drags his
quarry out of the
woods with a
stout cord and a
stick. Photo:
Wisconsin
Conservation
Department.

THE RIFLE

ety, but mule deer subsist from the desert to the Arctic, and provide as varied hunting as the habitats in which they live.

In appearance, mule deer, by and large, are stockier than whitetails and have larger "mule" ears. They have white on the tail, which is usually carried down, unlike the raised white "flag" so typical of the swiftly retreating whitetail. The antlers of mule deer and whitetail deer are different as well. In a typical whitetail stag, the antler grows as a single beam with the outcroppings or points branching from the main beam. With mule deer, however, each antler is likely to fork and continue to fork again, resulting in several beams, each with branches of its own.

18

The Ever-Popular Whitetail

The white-tailed deer *(Odocoileus virginianus)* is an animal that has managed to resist the encroachments of civilization amazingly well. From time to time it does suffer a population decline, but it has always managed to stage a comeback, and sometimes in surprising numbers. With sound management, the whitetail will be around year after year throughout most of its range.

The whitetail deer is not a big animal, but it has challenging proportions. It is adaptable to changing conditions. And it is wary; consequently it is usually available for hunting where other species have declined. Often the whitetail can be found right at the edges of towns and even cities. In fact, this deer seems to favor a semiwild type of terrain with mixed woodlands and marginal farmlands. It can be said that no hunter is really far from whitetail hunting in the U.S. If deer do not abound in one area, they can usually be found within a day's drive. There is no need, then, to travel far for good whitetail hunting. But year-to-year fluctuations in deer populations are critically examined by many wise hunters who wish to know if their chances of taking deer are better close to home, or whether they might better invest in an out-of-state license.

Whitetails are amazingly prolific, even near densely populated areas. In fact, more deer abound today than sixty or seventy years ago. Take a state like Illinois, for instance, with its growing, heavily urban population and intensive agriculture. Illinois has never been regarded as notable whitetail country. Yet its deer herd continues to increase, and its whitetails, fed on corn and browse, are bigger than the forest whitetails of northern Michigan or Maine. Even heavily populated New Jersey is known for its deer hunting. On the other side of the United States, you will find whitetails close to the apple orchards of Oregon, and they are so abundant in the brush country of Texas that hunters are allowed up to three deer per year.

Whitetail deer may not have the same appearance and size throughout the continent, but they are essentially one and the same animal. Those ranging from Maryland westward as far as Minnesota and up into Canada will usually be larger than the whitetails from Georgia, Missouri, or Texas. But they are basically the same animal and may be hunted by pretty much the same methods. There are, in fact, seventeen recognized subspecies of whitetail deer in the United States and Canada. From the hunter's point of view, they differ mostly in size. A rough rule of thumb indicates that deer in colder climates tend to be larger than those in warmer climates. Thus, you'll get a chance at heavier deer in Maine or Minnesota than you will in the Florida Keys.

In many parts of the country, the whitetail herd is still as vigorous as ever and is even increasing in numbers. But there are places where the deer have surpassed the food supply and are running into difficulties finding sufficient forage. In such critical areas, deer starve in winter.

As Americans, we like to think that hunting the whitetail is

The Ever-Popular Whitetail

an important national privilege—and it is. It is also a time-honored one, for deer hunting was of crucial importance not only to the American Indians who first lived on this continent, but also to the European settlers. It has been argued that the whitetail was more important—for its hide and meat—than the vast herds of buffalo that ranged across the country's central plains. Whitetails were hunted from the beginning, at times for survival of the colonists. Buffalo were hunted long after the settlement of this continent was secure. Up until the last century, market hunting of deer was so intense that the herds all but disappeared. A low in the deer population occurred around 1900, shortly after market hunting was outlawed. Since then, matters have improved beyond expectations.

Live-trapping deer and transporting them to places without deer but where the habitat was appropriate and the food ample, was a conservation measure that reestablished deer populations—and better hunting—in many states.

Trophy Whitetails

Needless to say, the true trophy deer is a rarity. Yet the head of almost any adult whitetail buck makes a handsome adornment to any wall. Some antlers are ragged and unsymmetrical in appearance, but they are interesting just the same, and certainly are proud mementos for any hunter. There are records of whitetail racks in which the main beams are over 31 inches in length—handsome sets of antlers indeed.

I have no doubt, though, that there have been even better-sized antlers than these among bucks that were never recorded. During the early logging days in Minnesota, Wisconsin, and Michigan, for example, exceptional deer were taken but never registered. Antlers didn't mean much. The deer were shot for the table and used as such. Many deer were shot for food for lumber camp crews. In those early days deer were abundant and easily taken. The camp cook got many of the

Whitetails are the most popular and prolific species of big game in North America today. Here a group feasts at a Maine meadow, not far from the woods where they can take shelter in an instant of alarm. Photo: Maine Department of Economic Development.

The Ever-Popular Whitetail

144

Although he doesn't sport a rack that would interest the serious trophy hunter, this buck looks like he'd provide a goodly amount of fine eating. Photo: Leonard Lee Rue III.

deer himself, often right from the cookhouse door or when taking a jaunt in the woods while the lumberjacks were cutting timber.

The Whitetail as Big Game

Whitetail deer, even the best-sized animals, are not really large in the proper sense of the word, despite their being big-game animals. When speeding along through the woods and really stretching their legs, they may look like a pony or even a small horse. A dead deer, however, is anything but this size.

The average whitetail ranges in height from about 36 to 42 inches at the withers. In length, the male whitetail runs from 60 to 75 inches with an average weight of about 160 pounds. Some large bucks will run into the 300-pound class, with the largest whitetail on record weighing 425 pounds. But these large deer are exceptions.

Geography mostly determines the deer's size. In southern Florida the deer are small, running in the 100-pound class. The Sonora whitetail, found in Mexico and Arizona, weighs little more. The deer in Minnesota, Wisconsin, Michigan, and parts

A whitetail doe on the alert in weedy cover. As soon as she picks up the presence of the photographer (or hunter), she'll be off like a shot. Photo: Leonard Lee Rue III.

The Ever-Popular Whitetail

of Canada are much bigger than this, although it is true that forest deer do not run as large nowadays as they did some years back when browse was more plentiful. The biggest deer today come from farming areas of the East and Midwest, where food is plentiful and of high quality.

Whitetail deer vary somewhat in coloration from one area to the next. In general, they are brown overall, shading off here and there to white. The color pattern changes somewhat with the season, but more in shading than anything else. The nose is black with a white fringe above it, and there is a large patch of white beneath the chin. The top of the tail is brown and the underside, along with the lower rear part of the deer, is a clear white.

Color shadings of the deer are especially noticeable in the spring and fall. In the spring the new coat is reddish brown in color, but in fall it shades into a blue-gray. The coloration as a whole is an aid to camouflage—a help in blending the deer with its background, to a remarkable degree, in any season. The winter coat is made up of long, thick hairs, which when cut in cross section and examined under a microscope look like sections of the insulating material known as Styrofoam. The hairs offer fine insulation against even severe cold. A whitetail deer can lie down in snow and make a bed so warm that the snow melts beneath it. The "sleeping quarters" of a herd in winter can often be discovered by the "pockets" of melted snow where the animals have bedded down.

Mature deer start growing their winter coats sometime in September or early October, and wear them until late spring. At this time they shed winter coats for the thinner and somewhat reddish coats of the warmer seasons. During the shedding period, the deer are shaggy and rough in appearance. But by spring they have a sleek and clean-looking coat again. New-born fawns have a reddish coat that is dotted with small white spots over the back. The spotting usually lasts only until fall, which is why a baby whitetail is called a spotted fawn. A doe's first litter usually consists of a single fawn. In subsequent years, twins are more common and triplets not unknown in areas where browse is abundant.

The most conspicuous feature of the whitetail deer is the large and bushy tail that is lifted high when the deer is surprised or starts running. As long as the deer is in motion, the white tail is held erect. It is dropped and the rump hairs bent inwardly when the deer slows up. The doe is especially quick to raise her flag, both as she flees from danger and as warning signal to her offspring, which are usually close at hand.

In the winter months, when bucks have shed their horns, the doe and the buck are hard to differentiate. Some woodsmen, however, claim that bucks exhibit more alertness. Fawns grow fast, and even when hardly a year old, they appear fairly well grown and able to fend for themselves. I have, however, seen twin fawns that preferred the company of their mother for over a year.

The Ever-Popular Whitetail

19

Natural History of
the Whitetail

In the Northern states, a doe carries her fawn or fawns about 204 days and bears them late in May or early in June. As a rule, a mature, healthy doe will bear twin fawns, occasionally triplets, and very rarely quadruplets.

Strange as it may seem, deer live in a matriarchy. That is, the doe is the head of the clan and lives separately from the buck, except during the yarding period in winter. In spring, the doe departs from the herd as a whole and finds a place of comparative seclusion where she can deliver and raise her young.

A healthy doe is capable of bearing fawns for most of her lifespan. She is never barren, except where bucks have been overhunted. Does have even been known to bear fawns until their death at 17 to 20 years of age, which is very old for a deer. Healthy year-old does will produce single fawns 30 to 40 percent of the time. At the age of 2 or 3 years, they will usually bring forth twins. This demonstrates dramatically that fawn production is the key to determining the future of a deer herd. Where you find a lot of fawns in the woodlands, you will usually find a healthy deer herd as a whole.

Where food and living conditions are adequate, fawns will be born and will keep contributing to an adequate deer population. Deer multiply fairly rapidly, especially where the does are well fed and healthy. The better nourished a doe is, the more fawns, within reason, she will produce and the better the chances are of survival for her offspring. How the female comes through the winter has much to do with the health of the fawns she will produce, and how they too will survive.

Some winters, especially in the Northern states, are severe and affect deer populations adversely. During winters that begin early and end late, deer frequently overbrowse their yards, become undernourished, and even starve. The deer that survive such conditions are in poor physical shape. The result is that many does become undernourished and cannot bear young.

Fawns born of half-starved does stand a poor chance of survival. Many do not even live a week. The newly born fawn lives on its mother's milk, nursing for several minutes every couple of hours. Fawns must have milk for about twelve weeks, after which they can get along on their own by browsing. Like mature deer, the fawn will eat tender shoots and leaves of annual plants during the summer, but will switch to twigs, buds, and leaves later in the season.

When yarding during the winter season, whitetail deer live mainly on whatever shoots they can strip from the trees. Where the trees are high, only the larger deer can feed satisfactorily, leaving many of the smaller deer to starve. The critical periods comes from December to April, when snows run deep in some parts of the country. Food must also be close to sheltered areas where the deer can seek protection from winds and falling snow.

At one time where browse was in short supply, bales of hay were set out as deer food by sportsmen. But to no avail. Deer

Natural History of the Whitetail

When snow gets this deep, the chances are that whitetails, such as this doe, will starve. The felling of small trees may help the animals survive such a winter. Photo: Leonard Lee Rue III.

have been found starved to death with bellies full of hay. In severe winters when deep snows prevent deer from finding herbaceous growth on the ground, it is far better to fell or bend over small trees such as birch or alder and allow even small deer to reach the topmost twigs.

After a winter in the deeryards, the whitetail's coat is thin, scraggly, and the animal itself is lean and scrawny. On close observation, the rib cage and backbone are noticeable. The deer as a whole appears to be in poor physical condition. At this time whitetails tend to congregate in small family groups, especially when feeding. They are quickly able to discover the

Late in the rutting season, when their antlers have turned white, whitetail bucks can often be found together where earlier they would have been jealously guarding their territory from other males. Photo: Leonard Lee Rue III.

Even when it's only twenty minutes old—as this one is—a whitetail fawn is able to stand by itself. Photo: Leonard Lee Rue III.

Natural History of the Whitetail

spots that hold any sort of available forage and congregate on them.

Little by little as the weather gets warmer, fresh forage and leaves begin to appear. Feeding becomes easier. The does especially appreciate the balmier days, for at this time they are heavy with young and seek solitude for the most part. Toward late May or early June, the does drop their newborn fawns.

The fawns are totally unable to fend for themselves at first and lie in some protected spot, such as high grass. With neck outstretched, they are virtually quiescent for the most part. They blend into their surroundings and are hard to spot. Once, while traveling along a trout stream, I came across such a newborn fawn. The little animal was so intermingled with its surroundings that its camouflage was nearly perfect. If I had not almost stepped on it, I would never have noticed it. What is even more amazing is that newborn fawns seem to, amazingly, have little scent. Even keen-nosed dogs have been known to pass by without notice.

As soon as newborn whitetails are able to use their legs (which occurs rather shortly—15 minutes or less—after birth), they are led by the doe to a fresh area where there is no odor of afterbirth.

During the whole summer, the doe and her fawns may prefer to remain in the vicinity of a river, stream, or lake. Not only is there plentiful succulent forage there, but brush also abounds for protection. There is, in addition, water to wade in when the flies become bothersome, especially during July and August.

When fawns seem to be in danger, they stay close to the ground as they run along and are often so concealed that they are barely visible as they travel. Fawns quickly discover that danger is always present, and take advantage of their small size, camouflage color, and if need be fleet feet to keep out of harm's way.

As the fawns mature, they remain in contact with the mother. But little by little they assert their independence. By midsummer you may see them all by themselves, especially during daytime. However, many remain right with the doe until fall and occasionally later. When the doe senses danger, the fawns take a quick clue from their mother. Should the doe snort in alarm and crash off through the brush, the fawns will follow.

Even in the fall, fawns will follow their mother and depend on her. One time, when hunting in November with deep snow on the ground, I saw one distressed half-year-old fawn come running through the woods bleating insistently for its mother. Somehow the fawn and the doe had become separated.

In summer, all whitetails feed as heavily as possible. By mid-August they are usually in good trim. The bucks are ready for the rutting season ahead and the does for the lean times of winter.

The doe, clearly, is the pivotal point of the herd. When the doe is ready to bear her young, she will find a place that she likes and will stay there until she has dropped her fawn or fawns, and perhaps for some time thereafter. After bearing her young, the doe will stay fairly close to a restricted range. She will travel, feed, and bed down in pretty much the same hide-out, as long as she finds it safe and there is sufficient food.

Natural History of the Whitetail

20

Trail Watching Pays Off

Before the deer season, whitetails are not as wary as they become when the guns begin to boom. Unmolested during the summer, they forget about such things as hunters. But when a nip in the air heralds the deer season, whitetails become much more vigilant. They start their morning meanderings along game trails before sunrise and continue after sunset. But the deer hunter who finds a favored spot on a well-used deer trail before dusk or dawn will stand a good chance of getting his venison.

Deer are always on the watch for movement. A hunter on a stand must sit absolutely still and let the deer come to him. It is a proven fact that hunters on stands see more game and get better, cleaner shots than hunters using other techniques.

Deer use certain trails or runways year after year. The trails always lead to good browsing areas. A good stand is where the game trail branches into a browsing area or into a bedding area of thick cover. When you approach your stand, settle down quickly. Make sure you are comfortable and can sit at your stand without moving for long periods of time.

Dress warmly. Be sure to have warm footwear. Warm woolen outer garments along with insulated, rubber-bottomed and leather-topped boots will usually assure you of keeping warm. Some hunters bring along a piece of tarp or a folding stool to sit on, or even drape themselves with a blanket. The stander must be patient and persevering. There is no way you can do this without being warm and comfortable.

You will do yourself a favor if you bring along a thermos of hot coffee and several meaty sandwiches. Time may pass slowly, and that coffee and lunch will make your vigil more comfortable. Many experienced deer hunters advise that lunch be eaten a distance from the stand, to avoid releasing odors that may be particularly noticeable to deer.

To become a good trail watcher requires a lot of patience. It may take a day or two for you to spot a deer. But in the long run it is rewarding. I know of one hunting party of five that spends a week at stand hunting every deer season, each at a different post. They all get their bucks every year, and they feel that the rewards are well worth the time and effort of a long watch.

The perennial stander is sold on his method. Some men find a favorite stump not far from camp and get to know everything in sight. Anything that moves is observed. Others study prospects from year to year and change their stands to suit conditions. But all know the value of patience, caution, the right time, the right place, and how to let the game reveal itself at close quarters.

With whitetail deer, however, nothing is dead certain. There will be occasions when deer approach but still keep out of gunshot range. You must remain both patient and absolutely motionless.

If the wind is blowing from the deer to the hunter, the whitetail may scrutinize the surroundings closely, sometimes even staring right at the watcher. It may then turn away, not overly frightened. Since a deer is color-blind, it cannot identify

Trail Watching Pays Off

a man by his clothing. Thus a person's bright hunting garb will look to the animal like a part of the scenery, as long as the wearer is motionless.

Sometimes a whitetail will travel along at a rather slow pace. But on most occasions it will move in like a silent shadow, pausing, raising its head, but always uneasy and restless. A deer does not depend on any one sense for identification of danger. It will verify with all of the senses if it can. It may take a few seconds to bring them all into play; enough usually for the motionless hunter to aim and fire.

The hunter who takes the time to learn all about the country and the habits and instincts of the deer that live there can usually predict what his quarry will do under most circumstances. When the hunter just goes out looking for a buck with no definite ideas, he is at a disadvantage.

A hunter must think like a deer. That means knowing what food is available, the lay of the land, and the influence of the weather at the time of the hunt. When the weather is blustery, with a lot of snow for instance, whitetails head for the parts of the range that are heavily wooded. Here they will make out the best they can for any available food, and not venture far. But they will be out searching for forage as soon as the weather clears. Study the deer's whereabouts by watching their trails and find out just how far they are travelling to feed.

Early in the morning, deer are anxious to leave more open browsing grounds and head for protective cover to spend the day. This is especially true when the hunting season is well advanced. By then the wise old bucks have taken on extra caution. I met one of these handsome and wary bucks on a stand this past season. It was just daylight, with the sun breaking out in a rosy glow. The light was poor when the deer showed up, and for a few brief seconds I didn't know if it was a buck or a doe. The buck was moving along steadily but slowly at first. Just when I saw its antlers, the big whitetail broke into a run and went scot-free. After one hurried shot and a miss, the buck was swallowed up by the nearby hemlocks.

THE RIFLE

My stand was in an area of fairly new slashings where deer like to feed and travel. It was a good place for a stand—fairly open with logging trails cut by fresh deer tracks. I missed the buck because I couldn't identify him fast enough. But deer are creatures of habit, and I'll get him yet.

The best stands lie along hills or high ground. Deer like to travel the ridges, so look for movement there. A whitetail does not always stand as a deer. Check for patches of brown and white, but look carefully to see if they do indeed belong to a deer. Watch especially for the telltale antlers. If a doe or two wanders into the area, be on the alert for a buck that might follow, especially during the rut, which frequently coincides with the hunting season in the Northern states.

Not all hunters like trail watching or have the temperament for it. It's not a pastime for an impatient man. It is, however, one form of hunting that the neophyte may find rewarding. And if he has the skill to find the right stand, the trail watcher sees nature in her many moods and can study the lesser wildlife around him. However, you must remain so still that squirrels and chipmunks virtually walk around you. You must blend in with the scenery and be accepted as part of it. When that happens, your chances of seeing and bagging game are favorable.

In selecting the right spot, try to evaluate your stand from a deer's point of view. Deer travel for the most part just before dawn and right after dusk. The hunter who is on a stand and warmly settled at these hours, facing upwind, will likely get action sooner or later. Places where deer tracks show that trails intersect is a clue for a good stand. A spot along the path where deer trails emerge from swamps and clearings is also worthy of attention.

What makes trail watching such a good technique is that the game will be moving while the hunter is still. This allows the hunter to take his time in shooting and thus perhaps shoot more accurately.

Oftentimes I find myself hiking through the woods and sud-

Trail Watching Pays Off

denly happen upon a location that seems ideal—a place that looks attractive to deer. Tracks and other sign will confirm this. Once I've proved to myself that it's the place I want, I stay there, even if I hear a barrage of shots suggesting that someone else is doing better. Shooting doesn't always mean hitting, and I've found that patience often pays off in the long run.

In the first part of the season, whitetails are not as wary and jittery as they become later on. So they move about more. When the hunting pressure is on, however, they travel out of the woods at the crack of dawn, heading from the swamps and thickets for quiet spots where they can feed, nipping at bushes and twigs, or bed down. They are much more wary.

There are plenty of crafty old bucks around who have lived so long because they are cautious. You can't get them by driving or stalking. Any sort of noise or human scent and they're gone. But being at the right spot when they choose to travel by is another story. As I said before, look for antlers, the black nose, or the white patch at the throat. A small part of the animal may be enough to alert you. Watch, especially, for that giveaway twitch of the white flag. Then raise your rifle when the deer's head is down. And do so very slowly. His tail will twitch just before he looks up. Make your shot before that happens.

When trail watching for deer, you will invariably hear shots. Other hunters' shots may be hard on your morale. Other hunters are evidently seeing game and not you. So you may decide to head out and look for a better stand. Don't! Roaming in the woods in a hit-and-miss fashion usually gets you nowhere. Stay put!

Trail watching in good deer country will pay off in the long run. By remaining at a well-used deer crossing, your chances of intercepting any passing whitetails are favorable.

Trail watching is a test of patience. It may be necessary to hold tight for several days. But for bagging a buck on a year-in, year-out basis, it can't be beat.

When the snow is on the ground is, obviously, the best time to ascertain where an active deer trail is located. Once the hunter has found his spot, he should pick a comfortable vantage point and wait for his opportunity. Photo: Michigan Conservation Department.

21

The Art of Stalking and Tracking

There is no more challenging way to hunt than stalking and tracking. Silence is the essence of the sport. You stalk steadily, studying tracks and signs. Are the tracks fresh, you ask yourself. You watch and listen as you travel, walking one step and standing for two.

By this method the hunter is able to cover a great deal of hunting territory. And if he's good at it, chances are he'll run across deer. The idea is to steal along as unobtrusively as possible, searching the region carefully for sight or sound of some whitetail buck in the vicinity.

Not only should the hunter walk on the slow and easy side, but at the same time he should head into or across the wind, for deer feed upwind as a rule. The whitetail has a highly sensitive nose—its first line of defense. By feeding into the wind, it is more likely to detect danger ahead.

The man who has trained himself to stalk very quietly—to

stop and look every so often—is likely to see deer. He must listen as well. Sometimes you can hear a deer run before you can see it.

As you stop and listen, try to sort out the usual woods sounds from those made by a traveling or feeding animal. In their daily wanderings, whitetails travel with a minimum of sound. But in brushy cover, they do make some noises such as the click of antlers against branches, the snapping of twigs, and even footsteps in dry leaves.

When a deer is feeding, there is always movement. The ears twitch, the tail twitches, and the head moves. All this can be detected by the rifleman.

If you feel you must get closer for a possible shot, look for any available cover and move only when the deer's head is down. Watch for the time the deer throws up its head or when it stops chewing its browse. It will be listening and watching then, so be still. Wait for it to feed again before moving.

To move almost noiselessly through the cover, you must have proper footwear. If the weather is mild, any soft-soled shoe will suffice, even tennis shoes. If there is snow on the ground, you will keep both your feet warm and your approach quiet by wearing rubber-bottomed, leather-topped boots. Your outer clothing should be of soft wool so that it will not make a scraping sound when touching the brush.

Pick your approach carefully when you suspect deer to be in the neighborhood. Keep bushes between you and the game, and when moving over a ridge or hill, do so gradually to ascertain quietly what is on the other side.

One of the best times to move into shooting range of a whitetail buck is when he enters a thicket to bed down. Start early in good deer cover and pick out fresh tracks to follow. Where bucks only can be shot, you can frequently identify the male deer's tracks by the toeing-out of the front feet. Also, the space between the front feet of a buck is wider than that between the doe's feet. Buck tracks will also sometimes show a drag mark in the snow. The tracks of a doe do not have a drag

The Art of Stalking and Tracking

mark. Some hunters also claim that a wandering track is more apt to be a doe; that bucks travel in a more direct path.

When you encounter a morning track, most likely the whitetail is heading for some loafing grounds. That's where you should go. But don't follow right on the track. Stick to one side.

Tracking is easily done after a snowfall, but much more difficult when the ground is bare unless it has been dampened by rain. After a snowfall, especially early in the hunting season, stalking deer is easier. The animals still have not lost their feeling of security and relaxation. A good time for tracking deer is during a snowfall. You know then that the track is fresh and the falling snow covers some of your walking sounds.

Even with good tracking snow on the ground, don't think that deer will be pushovers. You can read the signs and follow the tracks of a particular animal easier with snow present, but the whitetails are still cautious and require careful stalking for close-in shooting.

There is also the possibility, and it happens all too often, that after several inches of snow a thaw may follow, leaving a hard and noisy crust on the snow. With ice underfoot, stand hunting generally takes preference to stalking. However, I did walk into a big, handsome, antlered buck once when the forest floor was pretty much one solid sheet of ice. I dropped him as he broke into a slow run. Despite the crunchy ice, this whitetail did not hear me until it was too late. I was wearing rubber-soled boots that gave me just the edge I needed.

How you react when you happen upon browsing or bedded deer not far away is a real test of your skill and patience. This is the time for a slow and steady approach. The best idea is to keep well shielded, if at all possible, making no move while the whitetails are looking about. Lean against a tree and plan your stalk. It's best to wait until the deer have finished browsing and begin to bed down. Look for a spot ahead that allows clear shooting, for even a branch in the way can deflect a rifle bullet.

THE RIFLE

At times you will find a fairly good distribution of deer sign, and in such an event you will usually walk into a shot by just easing along, eyes on the woods ahead. Keep your eyes at deer level. A whitetail can turn up almost anywhere in a well-tracked bit of territory. Your best bet for a kill is to see the animal in time for a shot before it presents a vanishing white flag.

Windy weather can also work in your favor when approaching deer. A strong breeze rustling the treetops will help deaden your footsteps, and will enable you to hunt different terrain such as dry and crackly slashings. In many areas of whitetail country, there are sections of woodland which were logged at one time or other. The ground here is covered with branches and downed treetops. If the slashing is fresh, deer even like to feed and hide there. Hunting over this buildup of brittle branches is none too easy. But a good wind whistling through the brush and treetops will aid you in working close to the deer area.

As the hunting season advances, the bucks, by instinct, feel that they are being pursued. They will travel to their woodland retreat as quickly as possible every morning. Where bucks bed down for the day may also be a long way from where they feed. They may also be on the move much of the time, bedding down here and there for a few hours and up and moving at the first hint of possible danger.

If the rut is on, the bucks will also be in search of female companionship. Whether alone or in the company of a doe, however, that buck is a bundle of nerves once guns begin to boom in the woods on all sides.

If there are several hunters in the party, an effective method of approaching deer is to split up and circle some suspected bedding ground. One man takes the trail to the left that runs to the deer's location. Another takes the trail to the right, while one man can follow the main trail. The other members of the party should try to cut the deer off before it turns tail and vanishes into the woods.

The Art of Stalking and Tracking

164

If you know where the deer are likely to bed down, you may well have the luck to jump an eight-pointer, such as this one. Photo: Leonard Lee Rue III.

A buck will steer clear of open spaces as it travels. For example, when crossing a road, a doe may not move too fast in crossing the opening space, but the buck will usually sail over it in high gear. For year-in, year-out success, the hunter must know and recognize the most populated deer range, and concentrate his hunting there.

Once you narrow down the locality to a specific place, go out and scout it if you can. Study the trails. Determine where the deer go at night and then be on those runways first thing in the morning to intercept the moving game. Discover the freshly used runways and keep to them. A deer may turn off the runs from time to time, of course, but when traveling for some spot your whitetail likes the familiarity of known trails.

THE RIFLE

With deer nearby, stalk as close as possible before you raise your rifle. Keep the wind in your face and walk as if on eggs. A deer's sense of smell is better than its eyesight. But it can also see well enough at that, even with head lowered, for the eyes of a deer are so placed on both sides of the head that it can see in all directions even with the head down.

If a deer should get your scent only faintly, it will run its tongue over the end of its nose to dampen it. This sharpens the sense of smell. Somehow the scent penetrates better through a

Knowledge of the terrain is of great help in tracking deer. For example, if a fresh track leads in the direction of a source of water, you may well find the deer there, drinking. Photo: Leonard Lee Rue III.

The Art of Stalking and Tracking

moistened nose. When a deer gets a noseful of human scent, it will frequently snort loudly before taking off in high gear.

Some hunters, incidentally, claim that they can smell deer. Whitetails do carry a strong odor on occasion, especially when the pelt is wet. I have never been able to detect a deer this way, but I do believe that it is possible.

Successful deer hunters see the deer before the deer can see, smell, or hear them. Whether you are following a track or just hunting quietly and reading signs, keep your eyes searching for nearby game. Too many hunters keep their eyes on the ground too much. Deer aren't mushrooms. So even when tracking, keep your eyes up, glancing down only now and then for a fleeting second. Move slowly and quietly or you will either push the deer out far ahead or cause them to lie tight and allow you to pass by.

Big bucks are especially adept in letting the does run out ahead of them. When the does and fawns have drawn the hunter's attention away from the big buck he will either bound away in another direction or slink off, tail down, making no noise whatever.

When you suspect that deer are close, keep your rifle ready. If you're wearing thick gloves or mitts because of cold weather, take them off. I failed to get a shot at a well-racked buck on a very cold morning once because I was wearing heavy mitts and could not pull them off before the deer was gone. But then that's part of the game. If we got every deer we saw, hunting wouldn't be much of a challenge.

22

The Productive Deer Drive

Driving is an excellent means of moving and seeing whitetails. For hunters who don't have the patience nor the experience for stalking or tracking, the drive is the best bet. Both the Indians and the white settlers used the drive to bag venison for their winter larders. When the meat supply ran low, many of the early settlers counted on the neighborhood deer drives to keep them fed. Anyone owning a rifle or shotgun joined in, either as a stander or a beater.

The deer drive gives every hunter in the party a chance to participate in the hunt. The newcomer especially appreciates group hunting, because he knows his chances of collecting game are much better with a group of other hunters than when trail-watching or still-hunting on his own.

In order to make the drive a success, experienced hunters must lead or organize the event. In any group, some members must have prime knowledge of the country being hunted.

They must know where to drive and where to post the men on stands. The number of hunters in the party must depend on the size of the woodlots and covers being driven, and on the number of watchers needed. Generally, however, overly large drives are not very effective.

The element of safety must always be exercised for both drivers and standers. Standers, for example, must remain at their post throughout the hunt. It is unsafe to have men wandering in front of the drivers. This is also why a drive cannot be conducted in an area that already has too many hunters.

The most successful drives take in a rather small territory. Deer will keep on the runways only so long, and then will seek safety back past the drivers in nearby brush or thickets. Where the country is marked by ridges and hills, drivers have difficulty in keeping spaced and in timing the drive in an adequate

Here is good terrain for a deer drive. There is a ten-point buck in this photograph, but he'll be even more difficult to pick up in the wild. A drive will get him moving and give the alert hunter at least the opportunity of a shot. Photo: Leonard Lee Rue III.

fashion if the area driven is too big. A drive of some half mile in length is generally more successful than one twice that size. A drive of 300 or 400 yards is even better. If deer are to be driven in a stretch of a half mile or more, it is better to break the drive into smaller portions and cover each separately, if possible. Since correct timing is the essence of the drive, the smaller push becomes easier for everybody. And it produces more game.

The length and breadth of the area to be driven must be thoroughly planned and discussed before it is undertaken. The standers must be positioned in places where the driven deer are likely to pass. In many deer covers there are roads or trails that can be used for boundary lines. When the extent of the drive is determined, the drivers are notified when the drive will start. They must be on their stands before that.

The natural lay of the land must be taken into consideration when the standers are placed. They must be upwind of the drivers and in places that the deer will want to cross in order to reach some shelter beyond. The hunters must remember that the driven game is seeking security, and knows where that safe cover lies.

On his way to the stand, the assigned hunter should move as cautiously as possible and keep an eye out for game along the trail he is taking. He should approach his post with caution, and should a deer appear anywhere on route, he is entitled to bag it if at all possible.

Usually the more proficient hunters are the ones to make the drive. They must keep their eyes open for deer that try to break to the sides or try to sneak through. The drivers must maintain as uniform a line as they can, and make an effort to stay fairly close to one another. They should walk along at the same pace and keep the game moving ahead, if at all possible. Any deer that breaks to the side is fair game for any driver who spots it and can get it under his gun sights.

This buck is bedded down in high grass. Without a drive, the chances of finding him are very slim indeed. Photo: Leonard Lee Rue III.

An alerted buck going all out. In this situation, there is little excuse for not bringing home the venison. Photo: Leonard Lee Rue III.

The main concern of the drivers should be to bring the game close to the positioned shooters. But drivers may use any opportunity that presents itself to down any deer, as long as the shot can be taken with no danger to any member of the party. There is always a tendency for whitetails to turn back whenever they can. More than one good buck is taken by drivers each year.

When on watch, the hunters wait for the deer to reach good shooting range. They must not leave their stand at any time. As in any trail-watching procedure, there is always the temptation to scout the vicinity and see what's beyond the next bend. This is a mistake. A deer might pass one's stand when least expected. It is also a violation of basic safety procedures.

In driving, the most experienced drivers hold down the ends

The Productive Deer Drive

of the line where the deer have a tendency to slip away from the push. At one time drivers made a lot of racket by barking, whooping, and hollering. But this noise is unnecessary, and in some areas illegal. When a group of men walk through the autumn woods, there will be sounds enough to alert the deer and keep them moving toward the men on the stands.

Generally, the first drive of the day is the best. The deer have had the night to themselves and will be inclined to follow the natural runways when being moved. It is essential that the hunters assigned to the stands be at their stations before the drivers begin any drive.

Even if the drive does not get underway on time, the standers can keep watch over their posts for any stray deer that may turn up. This is something that can happen early in the morning when the game is usually traveling to its daytime hideout.

Another type of cooperative hunting that has found favor with many smaller parties is the hunt that combines driving and still hunting. Some groups of deer hunters like to go about the drive in a rather relaxed fashion.

After a bit of consultation and often some banter, the hunters decide on the area and then go out in a group. They work together in a slow, quiet drive, but pause frequently to look and listen. They may have some men on watches or they may not. The idea is to keep the whitetails on the move so that sooner or later a deer will expose itself to one of the hunters. It is the diversified action of this hunting technique that appeals to many riflemen and that often produces shooting where one hunter alone or even a couple of hunters might not be as effective.

Another type of deer drive is a drive with hounds. Here, the hounds are used instead of beaters or drivers, although a man or two may take the hounds through the cover that is being hunted. Deer driving with hounds is a big tradition in many of the Southern states, right into eastern Texas. But it is also legal in California and in the Canadian province of Ontario.

A deer drive with hounds is practiced in essentially the same manner as a deer drive with beaters. Men are posted on watches and then the hounds are turned loose in the area to be driven. A man or two may walk with the hounds or even ride through on horseback. But in some places even that is not necessary. The hounds know what to do and can get a chase going by themselves.

Hounds used for deer hunting are frequently one of the coonhound breeds such as blueticks, redbones, treeing Walkers, Plotts, black and tans, or even foxhounds. But often they are grade hounds of mixed ancestry. Curs and mongrels are used as well because they generally won't chase a deer for long. In small covers, a long-running hound will chase the deer right out.

This is also why beagles are used on deer in some areas. Beagles don't push deer too fast. In big swamps, however, only a large, fast hound is capable of putting enough pressure on a deer to make it run across an opening or road where the hunters on stands can get a shot.

Many Northern hunters believe that deer hunting with hounds is unsporting, but this is not so. Deer hunting with hounds in the Northern woods with the armies of hunters that are there during the deer season would be unsporting. But not in the Southern swamps. In many areas of the South, driving with hounds is the only practical way of hunting deer. The swamps are too thick for still hunting or stalking. In fact, men can not even walk through some of the swamps. So driving with beaters is impossible as well.

Deer hunting with hounds has an honorable lineage. In the South it was practiced by the very first settlers who brought deer hounds with them from England. Certainly deer hunting with hounds does not facilitate the overharvest of deer. Bag limits on deer in the South are very generous. Most states allow several deer per season per hunter. The lengths of the deer seasons are equally generous, as long as two or three months in some states.

The Productive Deer Drive

23

Tactics for Western Deer

When a hunter thinks of deer hunting in the West, his thoughts generally drift off towards big mule-deer bucks with rocking-chair antlers. But muleys aren't the only deer found in the West. The whitetail deer, for example, is surprisingly abundant in Montana and Wyoming, and is not hunted as much as it could be. Then, of course, there is also the small Coues whitetail of Arizona and New Mexico.

The western slopes of the Rocky Mountains have the blacktail deer, an animal that lives in a forested habitat much like the Eastern whitetail.

The mule and blacktail deer are one and the same species—*Odocoileus hemionus*. They are, however, different subspecies. The blacktail is, on the average, a smaller deer than the muley. As the name suggests, its tail is all black; the tail of the mule deer usually has only a black tip. But even the tail of the blacktail is small and inconspicuous when compared to the "white flag" of the whitetail deer.

The blacktail, being largely a forest animal, can be hunted with the same tactics as those used on the whitetail. Still hunting at a slow pace is a favored method. It's a good tactic because blacktail forests seldom have the hunting pressures of the Eastern woods. The deer are not as spooky and tend to stick to their habitual daily routines.

When still hunting for blacktails, it's a good idea to avoid the deep stands of the Pacific rain forests. The cover is thick and getting a shot is difficult. The hunter should penetrate far from roads and into the hills so that he gets away from other hunters. But he should stick close to openings—meadows, logged-over areas, old burns, and old logging roads. That is where he will at least have a chance for a shot.

Openings also tend to have more young trees and shrubs for good browsing. Thus they have more deer than the deep, mature forest. Blacktails, like all deer, tend to come out of the thickets to browse during dawn and dusk. A hunter after blacktails has to be out early.

Taking a stand on a well-used deer trail also has good possibilities. The hunting technique is again the same as trail watching for whitetails. Big drives are not popular with Western hunters, perhaps because this method of hunting is not needed. Hunters can score on their own. But small drives with three or four men—a couple driving and a couple on stands—are used in small covers and small forested ravines. Similar drives are also used on mule deer during midday when the muleys are bedded down. In California, dogs are occasionally used to hunt blacktails. The technique is similar to that used in the South, but generally two or three dogs are used, not entire packs.

Blacktails can also be hunted by calling. This method was practiced by the Indians. The hunter bleats like a lost fawn, hoping to attract adult deer coming to rescue the fawn. Calling during the rut is also practiced. In a way, this is similar to the "rattling up" of whitetail bucks accomplished by banging a set of antlers together. The rattling of deer is only practiced in

*A blacktail buck moves cautiously in a direction he thinks will
bring safety. Photo: Len Rue, Jr.*

Texas, while calling of whitetails only in the far Northwest. It
is not a popular hunting method and calls for a thorough
knowledge of deer habits.

It's the mule deer that makes up the backbone of Western
deer hunting, or at least the more glamorous part of it.
Perhaps one reason is because mule deer have much bigger
racks. But the main reason is that they also have a bigger range.
They are found in all of the Mountain states from Mexico to
British Columbia and eastward into Nebraska and North
Dakota.

Mule deer are mainly hunted by stalking and glassing. The
same technique, incidentally, is used on the diminutive Coues
whitetail in the hilly country of the Southwest.

Deer hunters who have hunted both whitetails and mule

deer will generally agree that muleys are easier to bag. There are a number of reasons for this. Mule deer are more wilderness-type animals than whitetails. Many parts of mule-deer range even today are sparsely settled. Thus mule deer have not been exposed to hunting for as long as whitetails, and not to as much hunting pressure. Consequently mule deer are not as nervous and jumpy as whitetails. They are more placid.

At the same time, they are more gregarious animals. This is of immediate advantage to the hunter. And, of course, mule deer are animals of more open country—of rolling hills. Many areas of mule deer range are not heavily timbered at all. The only trees and cover may exist at the bottoms of canyons and draws, or on the northern slopes which generally receive more moisture.

A rare sight anywhere—two spike blacktail bucks, fighting. Photo: Len Rue, Jr.

Tactics for Western Deer

All this makes mule deer hunting easier from the standpoint of success. To hike the mountains, however, a hunter must be in good physical shape.

Glassing and then stalking is one of the favorite methods of hunting mule deer. The hunter must be up in the hills. He begins to glass at the first light, hoping to see a deer either browsing or moving from a browsing area to where it will bed down. If a browsing deer is spotted and there is time to stalk, then a hunter should try to keep the wind in his favor.

In most cases, however, the deer will be moving. Here the hunter wants to follow the deer with his binoculars and attempt to learn where the deer beds down. Then he must make a stalk and jump the deer.

Hunters should be up high when glassing, not only because they will be able to see more countryside that way, but also because big old bucks tend to hang out higher up the slopes. Stalking downhill is also easier. The deer rarely look up the slopes for danger. They expect coyotes and the like from below, so they hide on the upward side of any cover. This makes them easier to spot from above.

The ideal places to glass for mule deer are high ridges overlooking valleys and canyons. Since the deer will be moving from more open country into thicker cover to bed down, a hunter should position himself so that he has a commanding view of likely bedding areas. When glassing, the hunter should not expose himself in the skyline. Mule deer have fine vision and they make good use of it.

By the time full daylight arrives, mule deer will have bedded down or taken to cover. By and large, only alarmed deer move about in full daylight. In the early fall when the weather is warm, the deer will bed down in places with plenty of shade. The cool, timbered basins and forested northern slopes are favored. Breezy heads of draws are also favorites. Mule deer like to bed down just below a ridge from which they can watch the valleys or canyons below. At the first hint of danger, they can be over the ridge and gone in a few jumps.

THE RIFLE

With the coming of cooler weather later in the season, the deer tend to bed down in places where they will be sheltered from cold winds and at the same time catch the sun's warming rays. Slopes with southern or eastern exposures are usually preferred at this time. The deer frequently bed down with low-lying evergreens behind their backs, out of the wind.

When the deer are bedded down during daylight hours, a hunter has no choice but to try to jump them out—to make them move and to move them in such a direction where a shot can be had. In areas where deer are plentiful, hunters have been known to ride on horseback along trails and make enough deer nervous that sooner or later one of them exposes itself for a shot. Certainly hunting on horseback is an easy way to hunt, and the hunter has the horse to carry out his deer if he is lucky enough to bag one.

But a man on foot has a couple of advantages. For one thing he can get into the action quicker if a big muley buck suddenly jumps up out of some brush. By the time a hunter on horseback dismounts and jerks his rifle out of a scabbard, the buck could be gone. The hunter on foot also gets into country that is too steep and rough even for a horse. Also, mule deer become more jittery and leave the cover more readily when confronted by a hunter on foot. Horses don't alarm mule deer as much as a man on foot.

A hunter trying to jump a mule deer from a bed should investigate every patch of brush or every clump of trees he can. Mule deer are used to hiding in small bits of cover. It is surprising how little cover they need. They can hide in clumps of brush that scarcely seem big enough to conceal a cottontail. In the northern Mountain States, aspen groves are one of the favorite places for mule deer to bed down. A hunter should investigate every one he can.

Trying to jump a mule deer out of its bed can be done by one hunter, but chances are that most deer will give him the slip. He won't even see them, because as he enters one side of a patch of cover, the deer will go out the other side.

Tactics for Western Deer

A mule deer doe with fawns moves across a meadow. Photo: Leonard Lee Rue III.

The mule deer, and its subspecies the blacktail of the Northwest Coast, sports antlers that differ markedly from those of the whitetail deer. Photo: Len Rue, Jr.

THE RIFLE

Here is a mule deer head that any hunter would be proud to display on his wall. Photo: Len Rue, Jr.

This kind of hunting is ideal for two or three hunters working as a team. One or two hunters work their way through the cover in a draw or canyon or on a hillside, while the third stays higher up. It is the hunter higher up who will see most of the deer and probably get most of the shooting.

Even when hunting rolling country, the hunters should split up and hunt two or three hundred yards apart. A deer moved by one hunter may offer another a shot. Deer have a one-track mind. If a deer is trying to elude a hunter, it does not anticipate another one. Hunters should always use a bit of strategy. They should choose their routes so that if they do move a deer, they will be able to shoot. This, of course, is not always possible. If one hunter goes into some heavy brush, his partner should be stationed where he is sure to see any deer that may move out.

Mule deer live in a variety of habitats, but always in semiopen country. You can find mule deer in the rolling scrub desert of northern Mexico, where it is warm the year around. You can also find them in the Canadian Rockies on hillsides covered with lodge pole pine where winter temperatures plummet to 30° below zero.

In the northern Mountain States, mule deer are migratory. Just before the deep snows of winter hit the northern slopes, the deer move down into the sheltered valleys where browse is more abundant and snows are apt to be less deep. The does and fawns move down first. The old bucks come last. Mule deer bucks always live higher up the slopes than does or young bucks. A hunter after a trophy has to go up high. In areas of mule deer range that also accommodate sheep— desert or California bighorns—big mule deer bucks can be as high up as the sheep.

A good time to hunt mule deer, particularly if you are after a trophy buck, is following a snowfall. Some states have late seasons so that hunters can hunt the deer that have come down from the mountains. Walking in deep snows is hard and horses cannot always be used, but late-season hunting can be very rewarding.

Many whitetail-deer hunters, seeing a mule deer buck run for the first time, believe that muleys cannot run as fast as a whitetail. This is not true. When a mule deer is alarmed, but also puzzled as to what has caused the alarm, it will run with a stiff-legged gait, bouncing and coming down on all four feet at once. This gait is not the best for a fast getaway.

A mule deer hopping like this is not hard to hit. And chances are that once it runs a short way—a couple of hundred yards perhaps—it will stop and look back.

When a mule deer is really frightened and knows what has frightened it, it moves with astonishing speed, particularly if it's running uphill. The back feet come up behind the front feet and push with great power. The deer simply glides over the ground.

Mule-deer bucks grow larger racks than whitetails. Eastern whitetail hunters are generally overwhelmed by the size of their racks. They see a mule deer buck with an 18- or 20-inch spread and they think: what a rack! It would be on a whitetail, but on a muley it's only so-so.

A good way of judging a mule deer's rack is to compare it with the deer's ears. The ears on a mule deer are about 11 or 12 inches long. When the rack extends several inches on each side of the ears, you know that you're looking at a good buck.

A rack on a running buck is much harder to evaluate, but if the rack extends beyond the rump outline on each side, you'd better get into action fast. This is a real wall-hanging trophy that any hunter would be proud to have.

Tactics for Western Deer

24

Buck Fever and Its Cure

Where the buck is first seen usually has a lot to do with whether or not it is downed. When a broad-beamed buck is seen at a distance, it probably does not grip the emotions as drastically as it does when the deer comes ambling along at close range and presents an easy target.

Buck fever is by and large a malady of tyro hunters. When a buck suddenly materializes, the novice realizes that this is his one good chance, and becomes so caught up in the excitement of the moment that he becomes hopelessly rattled. For example, while in the deer woods one balmy November morning, I happened to run across one of these neophytes who was so excited and overcome by what he had just experienced that at first his story was a jumble of words. All I could understand was:

"The buck was right there! The buck was right there! I missed him! I missed him!"

With trembling hands the young fellow pointed in the general direction of a patch of brush, where he told me he had seen two deer—a buck and a doe. In his excitement he managed to get off two shots, but even at the close range at which the deer were seen he had failed to hit the buck.

On another occasion I met one hunter who claimed that he had just fired every bullet in the chamber of his .30-30 at a standing buck and had missed with all of them. But I had not heard a shot. I knew that something didn't add up. So I began looking at the ground near where he stood. There were the results of his "shooting"—seven unfired cartridges strewn on the hard snow. The wrought-up hunter had gone through the mechanics of ejecting the bullets in his rifle, but had never pulled the trigger. He had worked the lever-action rifle in his hands for all it was worth, but had never fired a shot.

There are some beginners, on the other hand, who can take such situations right in stride. These imperturbable newcomers have never fired at a buck before, and should one appear it is a simple matter for this cool individual to raise rifle carefully, aim, and make a killing shot. I've always felt that some of these self-restrained riflemen are not too enthusiastic about bagging a deer. They don't care if they get one or not. It is the impressionable young hunter who has looked forward to the deer hunt for weeks and wants a buck so badly he can almost taste it who is most apt to get buck fever.

Buck fever can befall an experienced hunter as well. It may occur in a mild form, but even then it can mean missed deer. A hurried, flustered shot is likely to mean a missed deer. "If I'd just taken my time," is the way most men explain it.

"That big buck was just moving along in the open and I got so rattled seeing him that I forgot to release the safety quick enough," is the way one experienced hunter put it.

But experience is the best teacher. Usually some good arises from any such encounter. The next time the same hunter is likely to be a bit more deliberate in his actions on encountering a deer. He may still be excited, but his shooting performance is apt to be smoother and more coordinated.

Buck Fever and its Cure

One attack of buck fever is enough for any big-game hunter. To avoid it, the hunter must assure himself. He must build confidence in himself. He knows he must take time to aim. If a man is able to hit a 6-inch bull's-eye consistently at 50 yards on the range, he can do the same on a deer in the woods, especially if that target is as big as a whitetail buck.

186

Confidence in your shooting ability will go a long way in avoiding buck fever or its relapse. Master your rifle. The shot at a deer is no different than one on a target.

The successful deer huntsman must know how to shoot with accuracy even under tension. He must be able to take his shot quickly from an off-hand position. The man who has had a lot of practice on the rifle range and is generally able to make an accurate and quick shot is the man who will most often return with venison.

When you are shooting poorly on the rifle range, try to determine why. Perhaps you are flinching. Perhaps you've developed some bad habit.

A running shot is the rule in whitetail hunting. You may catch your buck in a standing position, but usually that buck will have spotted or smelled you first and is going away when you raise your rifle. Don't let him bluff you out of the shot. Aim ahead and let the shot connect. One way to become a good running-deer shot is to practice with a moving, cardboard-filled auto tire. Find a hilly practice range, start the tire rolling down an incline, and then take your shots at it on its descent. Vary the range. Make sure that your practice session is carried on in a safe place. When you find you can hit such a mobile target consistently, you will have no trouble when you spot that whitetail going away from you at a pretty good clip.

A further cure for buck fever is to get out before the season starts and familiarize yourself with the deer woods. Look around for whitetails. Determine where the deer are. Look for deer trails along creeks and lakeshores. Search for areas where deer like to cross the highways. During small-game season, get out in the field. You may hunt for grouse or rabbits, but you can keep your eyes open for deer and deer sign as well.

THE RIFLE

25

The Deer Hunter's Wardrobe

To hunt in comfort, you must have garments that are designed for the sport and the weather conditions at the time of the hunt. You may encounter spells when the weather will be as warm as a summer's day. But then the temperature may drop, or rain may suddenly turn to snow. A wise hunter has extra garments against such contingencies.

Keep warm, but not too warm. If you're dressed too lightly, you will have to keep moving to stay comfortable in cold weather. You will not be able to stay on a deer trail for long. On the other hand, if you're dressed for zero temperatures but the day is warm, you'll find yourself sweaty, unduly warm, and uncomfortable.

Dressing for the type of weather you'll encounter each day will enhance your hunting. Only when you are comfortable will you be able to take things in stride and come back with a feeling of a day well spent.

The Jacket

When looking for an appropriate hunting jacket, there is none more suitable for the chillier days of the deer hunting season than the hunter-safety bright-red or blaze-orange woolen outer garment, commonly called the "deer hunting coat." All too many daysin the fallare so nippy that one needs real warmth in a jacket. For this purpose, 100-percent wool is the answer. Wool is soft, comfortable, durable, warm, and makes no noise when you are walking through the brush. There is a snug feeling about wool. It is soothing to the touch. Wool will shed some rain and keep you dry and warm.

The deer hunting jacket, like all hunting apparel, should be loose fitting to allow freedom of movement.

Another fine all-purpose coat for deer hunting, if you don't like wool, is one of blaze-orange nylon-cotton construction, with 100-percent goose-down insulated body and sleeves. When choosing the size, make sure it is large enough to provide freedom of action.

The Trousers

Some hunters prefer breeches, others trousers. If your preference is for breeches, look for a material with a fairly hard finish that will wear well. Water-repellent poplin is durable, and when lined with wool flannel, as some of the best are, serves nicely even in rough going. Breeches must be easy fitting, with plenty of room in the seat and knees. You may also want leather patches on the inner knee for longer wear, although this is not a necessity.

If your hunting is done in colder weather and you want all-season wear, there are the durable and long-wearing Malone pants. These trousers are 100-percent virgin wool of specially woven yarns. Their dense fabric gives protection from the cold, resists tearing by briars and brush, and is rain- and snow-repellent. Malone pants come in 30- and 32-ounce fabric. For rugged duty as deer-hunting trousers, they are in a class by themselves. They have been on the market for more than 80 years and are among the finest outdoor woolen pants made.

Underwear

An excellent answer to easy-fitting comfortable underwear for the deer hunter in cold weather is the two-layer Duofold. The inner layer is a soft, absorbent, non-itch cotton. The outer layer is a heavier lamb's wool. Perspiration is absorbed by the cotton inner layer and evaporated through the outer wool layer. With long-sleeved undershirt and ankle-length underpants, this suit weighs next to nothing. Its two-piece styling also allows for full freedom of movement. When the weather is warm, of course, a T-shirt and shorts will suffice.

The Shirt

A light-weight gabardine shirt is best for all-around use. The second shirt (I believe in the layering principle of two lighter shirts rather than one thick one) should be of 100-percent wool. Insist on the all-wool garment, and be sure that it's cut full through the shoulders, arms, and body, with a shirt tail long enough to tuck around the waist.

Socks and Boots

Wear nylon socks next to the skin and a pair of wool socks over them on frosty days. Again, 100-percent virgin wool is recommended. The best socks are elastic-knit mountain wool, with reinforced heels and toes. Use an inner sole in the boot for warmth and for cushioning the feet.

The best boots for the deer hunter in dry weather are of

quality leather. They give sure footing, comfort, and long wear. When you try on the boots, pull them over a pair of woolen socks to make sure that the fit is right. As the hunter will be on his feet much of the day, fit is all important. More than one hunter has quit the deer woods because of unsuitable foot gear. The boots should be fairly loose with two pairs of socks. Walk around some in the shop to test them before buying. And when you make a purchase, break them in on short trips first.

The best leather boots are the 8- or 9-inch topped leather boots on the order of the Russell De Luxe or Herman Survivors. The lighter the boot, the easier the going. With proper foot gear, the hunter can stay on his feet most of the day with no discomfort.

You must remember, however, that leather is porous. Properly oiled leather is water repellent, but not waterproof. A good combination in wet weather or snow is a pair of leather-topped rubber-bottomed hunting pacs. The best have cushion-soft soles of genuine crepe rubber, oil-tanned chrome leather uppers, and a comfortable soft leather inset in the back. The originals were called Maine hunting pacs, while the insulated boot of the same type is now called the Canadian "Sorel" and is fully insulated throughout with heavy felt. Wearing a pair of woolen socks with the Sorels will keep the feet warm even in sub-zero weather.

Head Gear

The traditional bright-red or blaze-orange woolen cap with earflaps will prove a boon and a blessing for the deer hunter all during the season. When the days are sunny and warm, the cap can be worn with the earflaps turned up. When the weather is chill and cold, the earflaps can be turned down, at least far enough so that they cover the tips of the ears where the cold first is felt.

THE RIFLE

There are hunters who prefer a parka with a hood over the head, but this piece of head gear shuts off sound considerably, limits the scope of vision on both sides, and also creates certain distracting noises under the hood that can be bothersome.

Gloves

For most of the deer season, the hunter will need nothing more than lined leather gloves for easy handling of the rifle. Gloves of this type will usually keep the hands warm and fingers flexible. When the temperature is on the freezing side, there may be need for more warmth about the hands. What is preferable at this time is a pair of buckskin choppers with woolen liners that are loose fitting and can be slipped off instantly when a quick shot has to be taken.

Garb for the Western Deer Hunter

Until now, my remarks about clothing have been addressed to the Eastern hunter in the northern deer woods. But the advice applies to deer hunting anywhere with climatic conditions that are encountered during the deer season in Maine, Michigan, or Minnesota.

Western deer seasons, however, frequently begin earlier. And mule deer are generally hunted in open country where the need for soft, noiseless woolens is much less. Western deer hunters lean to denims for their hunting in warm weather. Many-times-washed blue jeans are soft and noiseless enough for any deer hunting.

For head gear, the cowboy Stetson is still popular. In colder weather, down-filled jackets and vests are popular. Although the rip-stop nylon in most down jackets is noisy when brushed against twigs and tree limbs, a mule-deer hunter does not need to be overly noise-conscious.

The Deer Hunter's Wardrobe

The Southern deer hunter also does not have to concern himself with warmth the way a deer hunter in the Adirondacks does. Standing on a deer stand in a Southern swamp, listening to the baying of hounds and waiting for a deer to be driven by may be a bit chilly in the fall air, but it's not likely to be frigid. Khaki or denim pants plus a warm shirt and a jacket are apt to be enough garb.

Personal Gear

Three things that should be carried by the deer hunter at all times are: a map, a compass, and a good knife. Discover before the hunt how the compass is used. In the woods, orient the map with the compass, and by locating your position on the map, determine your way back to camp.

I like to have a small whetstone with my knife in case the edge needs touching up. There is no need for a long-bladed knife to dress a deer. A 4-inch blade is ample, and even a 3- or 2½-inch blade will do the task well.

The only other equipment a deer hunter needs is a piece of sturdy rope to drag the deer out and to hang it with. Some meat bags may perhaps be needed as well. And, of course, no hunter should be without plenty of matches in a waterproof container. A Western deer hunter will need a pair of binoculars as well—7x35 to 9x35 are about the best. But even Eastern hunters, who hunt whitetails in farming country and on open ridges in the Appalachian hill country, will find binoculars useful.

There's no need to fill the pockets to bulging, but you will find that a sandwich or two and several candy bars will help keep you from becoming too hungry. They're also good for a lift to the spirits. Travel light, however, and come back from the hunt ready for a hearty supper with no lessening of the appetite.

THE RIFLE

26

Don't Get Lost!

It can happen to the best of woodsmen. You suddenly lose your bearings. You can't tell how to get where you want to go or how to get back. In short, you're lost.

Most hunters in such circumstances get straightened out on their own in short order and without serious mishap. They're usually able to work their way out to familiar surroundings. But some deer hunters have met with tragedy and even lost their lives on becoming lost.

If you find yourself lost, the first few minutes can be the most crucial. Don't panic. Sit down on a log and reassure yourself that it's going to be all right. Do something soothing, such as lighting your pipe or eating a sandwich. Try to reconstruct how you got to where you are. Consult your map and try to identify any prominent landmarks which might allow you to orient yourself.

When snow blankets the ground, the problem is usually an easy one. Follow your footsteps back to camp or to the car. But if the ground is bare, a compass can be a lifesaver. Even a good compass is relatively inexpensive, and one should be carried on the person at all times. The best place for it is in the left breast pocket, tied to the coat lapel. Here it is always ready for quick reference.

It is best to play safe from the start. Check your directions from time to time when in unfamiliar terrain. Remember landmarks. Make note of them as you travel. Each one has a meaning and should be of help. But even so, if the hunter is not sure just where he is or where he's heading, check with the compass.

Here is a handy compass for any outdoorsman. The lanyard holding it fits comfortably around the neck where it hangs, unobtrusively, for easy access in case of need.

Once the hunter has oriented himself on the topographic map, he can use his compass to plot out the route to where he wants to be.
Photo: USAF.

THE RIFLE

A handy device for the hunter is this combination consisting of match holder, compass, and stout police whistle for summoning help.

For the hunter who is going off into wilderness areas—especially if they are unfamiliar ones—a survival kit is an excellent idea. Shown is a commercially made one containing a number of items that might well save a life. Many deer hunters like to carry a small rucksack to hold such things as survival kit, extra ammunition, or whatnot. Photo: Research Laboratories.

Don't Get Lost!

Do this every so often in strange territory. Between a study of known landmarks and a glance at the compass from time to time, you ought to be able to find your way in the woods with ease. Never quarrel with the compass either. A reliable make is always right—the compass needle will always swing to north.

Learn to read your compass properly before heading into the woods. When on the trail, go through some tests to make sure you're able to handle it. For instance, when starting out from camp, one usually has a definite hunting area in mind. Try to plan the distance to be traveled, estimate how long it will take to get there, and determine what direction this place is in relation to the camp or car.

Always carry a watch, too, and check it every so often. That way you'll know if you're overstaying your time or traveling too far.

By all means, learn to orient yourself in relation to the starting point. Let's say that the goal, Basswood Lake, is two miles southwest of camp. How long it takes to reach the place depends on the terrain and the way one hunts. But you know that when you get there you will have to travel in the *reverse* direction to hit your jumping-off place, and that will be northeast.

Trail crossings may be confusing at times, in which case I usually mark them with broken branches or twigs placed right on the trail. Let's say I come to a certain unfamiliar trail crossing. Which one did I come from? I place a couple of broken branches or twigs on the ground here, pointing my way out.

I always make a mental note of the time required to reach my proposed destination. This, together with the direction, will furnish me clues as to where I am and how long it will take me to reach camp. *Time* and *direction* are important travel factors.

In strange country, it pays to carry a small map of the area—one that you have studied in camp and on which you have noted landmarks and directions, especially in relation to camp. Along with this, carry a topographical map of the area. Such a map can be obtained from the U.S. Geological Survey, Department of the Interior, Washington, D.C. 20240, for a small fee. It will show you in detail the landmarks of the country in question, such as hills, swamps, lakes, streams, trails, railroads, and even outposts and other buildings.

One thing to remember is that a waterway will generally lead to some habitation. Make certain which way the water is flowing, and then work your way down, keeping a certain distance from the stream to avoid the tangles that usually mark the bank. Once the waterway leads you to people or habitation, directions can be obtained.

If you must stay in the woods overnight, find a sheltered spot and make a fire. This will be your campsite for the night, and once you have a blaze going you'll find that at least you can warm up and keep fairly comfortable. There will be wood to burn. The best kindling is usually dead branches at the bases of trees, especially evergreens.

If possible, build the fire against an embankment or near a bed of large rocks—out of the wind. This wind-break will reflect the heat back against you and help you make the most of the fire.

Once the blaze is going strong, add firewood gradually to keep it going. With the fire burning well, you'll find that you're feeling better and getting over any case of bad nerves that might have developed. Building the fire also helps you to keep busy. From then on you can settle down for the night and sit close to the fire to keep warm. This is also a time for you to gather your thoughts and figure out the course for tomorrow; that is, if you're not found during the night.

Keep the fire going. Its column of smoke will pinpoint your location for rescue parties. If you should leave the campfire, mark your way with blazes on trees so that you can return if you're unsuccessful in locating the way out.

In all this time, however, your companions will have sent out the alarm, and some authorities—the sheriff, perhaps, or the state police or forest rangers—will be looking for you. Aircraft may even be out searching, and your fire will give them something to spot, especially if it is emitting plenty of smoke.

Don't Get Lost!

The international distress signal is three of anything—three whistle blasts, three gunshots, and so on. In our deer hunting group we have a prearranged signal of three shots, ten seconds apart, at dusk. That signal means that you are lost. None of us has ever had to use it, but it's there.

The main thing for a lost hunter is not to panic and to stay near the fire. Don't wander off or the search party will have a much harder time finding you. Remember, there is nothing out there that can hurt you except your carelessness. A lost hunter can live for days without food.

27

Gun Safety and Sportsmanship

Courtesy is something that the hunter cannot leave at home. Consideration for the safety and feelings of one's companions in the field is just as important as it is in the city, and perhaps even more so.

Basic Rules of Conduct

Where a man may be hunting alone, he must observe certain basic rules of conduct for his own sake as well as for that of anyone else who might be in his vicinity. And when hunting in the company of others, the code is even more urgent. These rules amount to nothing more than fair play. The man who fails to observe them, especially in the handling of his gun, will soon find himself without hunting companions.

This code is based on nothing more than common sense and

tact, the result of inherited or cultivated good breeding. The hunter may be the best of shots, but if he is lacking in courtesy in the field, he cannot be classified as a sportsman.

Competition in hunting seems to be on the increase. Nonetheless, there is no excuse for poor sportsmanship.

Careless Hunters

It is true that some hunters never learn. One of the worst offenders is the man who handles firearms with no respect for the gun or his companions. Some men seem to have a superficial knowledge of firearms and look upon their weapons as if they were toys, which they certainly are not. Such a person may pick up any gun in camp without a care as to where the muzzle is pointing. There is also the man who is always ready and willing to offer advice. He seems to know all the tricks in the book. Yet should some hunter bag more game than he, congratulations are rarely forthcoming.

Always handle your gun with respect. I do not tinker with guns unless I check and recheck to see if they are loaded. Nor do I store my guns unless I make doubly sure that they are unloaded. It so often happens that it is the "unloaded" gun that causes the accident. Don't handle any gun until you take the shells out. Then check it again to make sure it's empty.

Etiquette

It does pay to be a good sport and try to get along with your hunting mates. There will be plenty of times when you can help your partner. If things are not going his way, try to build up his morale. Don't emulate the man who takes all the shots.

Give your companion his share of the shooting. Try to help him get close to the deer so that he, too, can get a shot. When

A buck in the wild is such an awe-inspiring sight that many hunters—even experienced ones—somehow choke up with that classic condition, buck fever. Photo: Leonard Lee Rue III.

your partner is getting his share of the shooting, he will be glad to hunt with you again. If you get a deer before he does, stick with him until he scores too, if at all possible.

By all means, if a young hunter shows interest in the sport, include him in the hunting party. Take him out before the season and show him the deer woods. Let him tramp the trails with you. Familiarize him with a rifle. Show him how to handle it with care, and how to shoot it accurately and safely. Make him feel at home in the deer woods, and you have a deer hunter for life—one that will be forever grateful for your companionship and advice.

Safe Gun Carry

Some experts advise that a firearm should be carried over the shoulder in the right hand with the barrel resting on the shoulder, trigger guard up. There is nothing wrong with this carry. However, the most comfortable carry I have found, which is also safe, is with the gun cradled under the right arm, with the right hand on the grip and the muzzle pointing at the ground.

As the gun is swung to the shoulder, the safety is released and the gun aimed at the target quickly. Under all circumstances, however, the gun is carried with the safety catch on.

Gun Safety

Being careful with guns means not only being careful not to injure yourself, but also to guard against injuring your companions. Make sure that your firearms are in top condition when setting out afield, and then handle them with care and safety both for yourself and your comrades.

This advice should be heeded by every shooter in the field—newcomer or expert. Figures show that almost a million new hunters are moving into the shooting field. It is sad that ever so many of them do not have the proper schooling to handle guns carefully. Many of them are not concerned in the safety of the sport, and even when given instruction in handling guns pay little attention to it.

It is no wonder that casualities result. Many of the accidents happen when the gunner does not see his companion. The victim might have been a partner who was near at hand when the hunter swung on the game in his companion's general direction. Some shooters mistake their companions for game. They hear a rustle in the brush and shoot.

Be careful with your gun when close to any human being. It is a proven fact that in half of all hunting accidents the gun and the victim are separated by a distance of ten yards or less! Most dangerous, then, are the hunter's own guns and the guns of his companions. Remember, always keep the muzzle pointed in a harmless direction!

Regarding the close-at-hand accident, statistics show that in Michigan in one period of 10 years, 76 Michigan hunters were mistakenly shot for game. But in the same period, 234 were shot by accidental discharges through horseplay, tripping, dropping guns, carrying loaded guns in cars, stepping into the line of fire, loading and unloading guns, cleaning guns, and just plain carelessness. Be careful and choose your companions carefully. In this way, none of you should join these statistics.

Gun Safety and Sportsmanship

Appendix: State and Agency for Hunting Information

ALABAMA
Dept. of Conservation
  and Natural Resources
Game and Fish Division
64 North Union Street
Montgomery 36104

ALASKA
Dept. of Game and Fish
Subport Bldg.
Juneau 99801

ARIZONA
Game and Fish Dept.
2222 W. Greenway Road
P. O. Box 9099
Phoenix 85068

ARKANSAS
Game and Fish Commission
2 Capitol Mall
Little Rock 72201

CALIFORNIA
Dept. of Fish and Game
1416 — 9th Street
Sacramento 95814

COLORADO
Division of Wildlife
6060 Broadway
Denver 80216

CONNECTICUT
Dept. of Environmental
    Protection
Wildlife Unit
State Office Bldg.
165 Capitol Avenue
Hartford 06115

DELAWARE
Dept. of Natural Resources
    and Environmental Control
Division of Fish and Wildlife
Tatnall Bldg., D Street
Dover 19901

FLORIDA
Game and Freshwater Fish
    Commission
Farris Bryant Bldg.
620 South Meridian
Tallahassee 32304

GEORGIA
Dept. of Natural Resources
270 Washington Street, S.W.
Atlanta 30334

HAWAII
Division of Fish and Game
1179 Punchbowl Street
Honolulu 96813

IDAHO
Fish and Game Dept.
600 S. Walnut
Boise 83707

ILLINOIS
Dept. of Conservation
Division of Wildlife Resources
605 State Office Bldg.
Springfield 62706

INDIANA
Division of Fish and Wildlife
607 State Office Bldg.
Indianapolis 46204

IOWA
State Conservation Commission
Information and Education
    Division
300 — 4th Street
Des Moines, Iowa 50313

KANSAS
Forestry, Fish and Game
    Commission
P. O. Box 1028
Pratt 67124

KENTUCKY
Dept. of Fish and Wildlife
    Resources
Capitol Plaza
Frankfort 40601

LOUISIANA
Wildlife and Fisheries
    Commission
400 Royal Street
New Orleans 70130

Appendix

MAINE
Dept. of Inland Fisheries and
  Game
State Office Bldg.
Augusta 04330

MARYLAND
Dept. of Natural Resources
Rowe Blvd. and Taylor Ave.
Annapolis 21401

MASSACHUSETTS
Dept. of Environmental
  Management
Division of Fisheries and
  Wildlife
100 Cambridge Street
Boston 02202

MICHIGAN
Dept. of Natural Resources
Mason Building
Lansing 48926

MINNESOTA
Dept. of Natural Resources
Division of Game and Fish
390 Centennial Bldg.
658 Cedar Street
St. Paul 15155

MISSISSIPPI
Game and Fish Commission
P. O. Box 451
Jackson 39205

MISSOURI
Dept. of Conservation
North Ten Mile Drive
P. O. Box 180
Jefferson City 65101

MONTANA
Dept. of Fish and Game
Helena 59601

NEBRASKA
Game and Parks Commission
P. O. Box 30370
Lincoln 68503

NEVADA
Dept. of Fish and Game
P. O. Box 10678
Reno 89510

NEW HAMPSHIRE
Fish and Game Dept.
34 Bridge Street
Concord 03301

NEW JERSEY
Division of Fish,
  Game and Shellfisheries
P. O. Box 1809
Trenton 08625

NEW MEXICO
Dept. of Game and Fish
State Capitol
Santa Fe 87501

NEW YORK
Dept. of Environmental
  Conservation
Division of Fish and Wildlife
50 Wolf Road
Albany 12207

NORTH CAROLINA
Wildlife Resources Commission
Albemarle Bldg.
325 North Salisbury Street
Raleigh 27611

NORTH DAKOTA
Game and Fish Dept.
2121 Lovett Avenue
Bismarck 58501

OHIO
Division of Wildlife
Dept. of Natural Resources
1500 Dublin Road
Columbus 43212

OKLAHOMA
Dept. of Wildlife Conservation
P. O. Box 53465
Oklahoma City 73105

OREGON
State Game Commission
P. O. Box 3503
Portland 97208

PENNSYLVANIA
State Game Commission
P. O. Box 1567
Harrisburg 17120

RHODE ISLAND
Dept. of Natural Resources
Division of Fish and Game
Veterans Memorial Bldg.
Providence 02903

SOUTH CAROLINA
Wildlife and Marine Resources
  Dept.
Division of Game
1015 Main Street
P. O. Box 167
Columbia 29202

SOUTH DAKOTA
Dept. of Game, Fish and Parks
State Office Bldg.
Pierre 57501

TENNESSEE
Game and Fish Commission
P. O. Box 40747
Nashville 37220

TEXAS
Parks and Wildlife Commission
John H. Reagan Bldg.
Austin 78701

UTAH
Division of Wildlife Resources
1596 West North Temple
Salt Lake City 84116

VERMONT
Fish and Game Dept.
Montpelier 05602

Appendix

VIRGINIA
Commission of Game and Inland
  Fisheries
P. O. Box 11104
Richmond 23230

WISCONSIN
Dept. of Natural Resources
Division of Fish and Wildlife
P. O. Box 450
Madison 53701

WASHINGTON
Game Dept.
600 North Capitol Way
Olympia 98501

WYOMING
Game and Fish Commission
P. O. Box 1589
Cheyenne 82002

WEST VIRGINIA
Dept. of Natural Resources
1800 Washington Street
East Charleston 25305

Canada

Information on hunting in Canada is dispensed by the provincial tourist departments. For general travel information, write to the Canadian Government Office of Tourism, 150 Kent Street, Ottawa, Ontario K1A OH6.

Tourist Services Division
Newfoundland Dept. of Tourism
5th Floor, Confederation Bldg.
ST. JOHN'S, Newfoundland
A0K 3E0

New Brunswick Dept. of
  Tourism
P. O. Box 1030
FREDERICTON, New Brunswick
E3B 5C3

Tourist Information Centre
P. O. Box 940
CHARLOTTETOWN, Prince
  Edward Island
C1A 7M5
Nova Scotia Dept. of
  Tourism
P. O. Box 456
HALIFAX, Nova Scotia
B3J 2R5

Québec Dept. of Tourism, Fish &
  Game
Place de la Capitale
150 Est Boulevard Saint-Cyrille
QUEBEC, Québec
G1R 2B2

Ontario Ministry of Industry and
  Tourism
Travel Services

3rd Floor, Hearst Block, Queen's
  Park
900 Bay Street
TORONTO, Ontario
M7A 1T3

Dept. of Tourism, Recreation &
  Cultural Affairs
Tourist Branch
200 Vaughan Street
WINNIPEG, Manitoba
R3C 0P8

Dept. of Tourism
Government Administration
  Bldg., 2nd Floor
REGINA, Saskatchewan
S4S 0B1

Travel Alberta
10255 — 104 Street
EDMONTON, Alberta
T5J 1B1

Dept. of Travel Industry
1019 Wharft Street
VICTORIA, British Columbia
V8W 2Z2

TRAVELARCTIC
Government, Northwest
  Territories
YELLOWKNIFE, Northwest
  Territories
X0E 1H0

Yukon Dept. of Tourism &
  Information
P. O. Box 2703
WHITEHORSE, Yukon Territory
Y1A 2C6

Index

213

Index

INDEX